Physical Education for
Children with
Special Educational Needs
in Mainstream Education

Physical Education for Children with Special Educational Needs in Mainstream Education

ISBN 1 871228 03 4

First published 1989 by **The British Association of Advisers and Lecturers in Physical Education**

Designed, produced and distributed on behalf of BAALPE by **White Line Press**, 60 Bradford Road, Stanningley, Leeds LS28 6EF. All orders to be sent to White Line Press.

Printed and bound in Great Britain.

Physical Education for Children with
Special Educational Needs
in Mainstream Education

BAALPE
British Association of Advisers and Lecturers in Physical Education

Contents

Preface

This book is the product of a working party which the British Association of Advisers and Lecturers in Physical Education established in 1987. This was in response to numerous requests for practical help which had arisen since the implementation of the 1981 Education Act. The working party met regularly for two years to produce the support material contained in this book. Consultations have taken place with colleagues, heads of school and teachers generally, to ensure not only the accuracy of the statements, but also the practicalities of the suggestions and recommendations. The book is presented in the hope that it will ease the burden of many teachers and improve the quality of the physical-education experiences offered to all pupils.

Members of the working party

Mrs R Barnett (Convenor)	Formerly Senior Lecturer in Physical Education and Professional Studies in Education, Bulmershe College of Higher Education, Reading
Mr J D Hall	County Inspector for Physical Education, Kent
Mr G B Kirkby	Senior Adviser for Physical Education, Lancashire
Miss R Makin	Adviser for Physical Education, London Borough of Redbridge
Miss D M Price	Senior Lecturer in Movement Studies, South Glamorgan Institute of Higher Education
Mr D H Williams	Formerly County Adviser for Physical Education, Cleveland

Acknowledgements

The BAALPE Working Party wishes to acknowledge the help gained from the following. We are most grateful:

● for the help and guidance given by teachers, advisers and physiotherapists;

● for clerical assistance from the Redbridge Education Services and from Bulmershe College of Higher Education;

● for the inspiration we have gained from the following writers:

J Male & C Thompson; *The educational implications of disability*; RADAR (Royal Association for Disability and Rehabilitation) 1985

Robert J Price; *Physical education and the physically handicapped child*; Lepus 1980

Lilian Grove et al; *Physical education for special needs*; Cambridge University Press 1979

Sheila Jowsey; *Physical education for children with a physical handicap*; Northamptonshire County Council 1984;

● for the considerable amount of work associated with the computer disk accompanying this book:

Helen Lane, Special Educational Needs Support Service, London Borough of Redbridge.

Computer disk

Included with this book is a Viewdata-style database of information relating to the various handicapping conditions. This database is on an 80-track double-sided disk for use with any BBC Micro or Master computer.

Introduction

The philosophy of this book

'Learn to move — move to learn' — such a simple phrase, but one of paramount importance to a child's normal development, especially a handicapped child.

At some time in their school lives most children, whether recognised to have disabilities or not, will have special needs. Learning to identify and satisfy these needs, which are often quite specific, is the physical education teacher's task. The reward is seeing each child attain his or her full potential.

All children with special needs should take part in regular physical education lessons, an area of experience which is vital to their growth and development. Often a handicapped child needs more, rather than less, physical education.

Children with a physical or sensory handicap can be particularly prone to lack of confidence in body management, which in turn can lead to further retardation of their overall development. Immobility due to paraplegia and other conditions often brings increased weight, making movement of any sort progressively harder. At the same time physical form and stamina become even more necessary in order to keep pace with everyday living. Fitness is essential.

Physical education does not serve physical purposes alone; pleasurable, interesting and creative experiences are all encountered through physical activities. For handicapped children the way to a free and independent life is not only through being well cared for, but also through learning to care for themselves. Children who are able to join with friends in their games and active pastimes are less likely to become frustrated or emotionally disturbed. In integrated education a child with special needs gets this chance and is encouraged to use it to the best of his or her ability.

The specific aims for physical education

Before planning any area of work it is essential to identify the precise aims and objectives one is trying to achieve. These will derive from a personal philosophy of physical education as well as from the philosophy of the school concerned.

It is generally agreed that a properly structured physical education programme should contribute to the following main areas of development:

Physical development

● healthy development of the heart, the circulatory system, the lungs, muscles and joints

● heightened awareness and control of the body

● development of coordination and skills

● realisation of full movement potential and learning the use of movement towards purposeful and creative ends

● improvement of stamina, suppleness, endurance, strength and fitness

● promotion of a positive attitude towards health and hygiene

● creation of an awareness that physical activity is for life, and is also fun

● learning how to make use of increased leisure time — an important factor for future generations

Social and emotional development
Throughout the physical education programme, situations will arise (or can be created) where attention can be paid to the following:

● cooperation and sensitivity towards others

● competitiveness and awareness of self

● taking responsibility, leading and following

● facing success and failure

● sticking to the task; learning to persevere

● recognising authority and learning acceptable codes of behaviour

● learning and developing a mature attitude towards safety

● building confidence in one's own ability and in the ability of others

● encouraging resourcefulness

● developing quality in performance standards

● encouraging decision-making

Intellectual development

Naturally, physical education classes focus primarily on physical activity, but they also present many opportunities for reinforcing skills common to other areas of the curriculum. These skills include:

● language and the communication of ideas

● numeracy

● perception

● problem-solving

● judgement

The goal for pupil and teacher is to strive together to improve and enhance the child's lifestyle. A positive view is essential: teachers who assume that physical education is not suitable or necessary for handicapped pupils will find that their expectations of the children's capabilities may be at an unfairly low level. A positive view, on the other hand, will result in great satisfaction for both teacher and pupils.

Chapter One
A Child's Development

This chapter deals with the sequence of physical development encountered in children. It is important that teachers who are responsible for planning a physical education curriculum have a basic knowledge of patterns of normal growth, and understand what is meant by good early movement experience.

The primary aim of physical education is to help the pupils to develop their physical skills in all areas, whether at home, at work or at play. Skill may be defined as:

> *The learned ability to bring about predetermined results with maximum certainty, often with the minimum outlay of time or energy, or both.*

To develop this ability children need to *explore, discover, repeat* and *elaborate* their early movement experiences. Practice and feedback are of paramount importance.

1.1 Motor development
Motor development and skill acquisition are sequential and continuous processes. Understanding how they function is critical for planning work tasks and diagnosing problems.

The normal sequence of events in motor development tends to follow a pattern:

● *reflexive* movements (non-voluntary) give way to *voluntary* movements, ie movements controlled by the child

● control is gained first of the *head*, and gradually moves down to the *toes* (top to bottom)

● muscular control starts by being more effective in the *middle* of the body before moving outwards to the *extremities*

● the clusters of muscles known as the *gross motor* muscles, controlling movements such as bending over and running, begin to function efficiently before the *fine motor* muscles, which control more precise and variable actions: for instance, the fingers picking up a small object, the use of the mouth in speech, eye movements, etc

Sensory motor experiences help to make sense of our lives. Touch, taste, smell, sight and hearing are the five immediately recognisable processes, but the sense of movement (*kinaesthesia*) is just as important, yet so often forgotten.

In order to achieve effective growth and development, the child progresses through a definite series of movements and activities within given periods of time, thus laying the foundation for much of its later learning.

Guidelines
Special-needs pupils may not precisely match the usual development pattern, but they should be given the opportunity to follow it as closely as possible.

Ideally children should be taught physical activities in groups where there is similarity in developmental age rather than chronological age.

1.2 Stages in development

Nursery/infant (age 2–7 years)
For children with special needs, the early years at school are extremely important. Not only do they have to learn to cope with locomotor and coordination problems associated with their handicap, but they also often have to catch up on missed sensorial and motor experiences. Consequently, while still learning to move, they also need to move to learn. Able-bodied children learn through play and exploration of the environment, but handicapped children are often less free to do this. For sensori-motor development to take place, they need well-structured and challenging opportunities in varied play situations. Communication skills should also be stimulated, thereby enhancing concept formulation and contributing to later learning.

Junior (age 7–11 years)
At junior level, special-needs children are becoming adjusted to the limitations in locomotion and coordination imposed by their handicaps. This is a time for them to develop their strengths and to compensate for their weaknesses. The movement education programmes should continue, increasing the range and choice of movements available, and the importance of games should not be overlooked. Games introduce many new activities, and although children of this age often find it difficult to relate well to others in a team, the skills and techniques of team games can still be developed. These foundations can then be built upon when greater social maturity is achieved.

Secondary (age 11–17 years)
As most special-needs children enter their teens, major team games and the refinement of individual skills become more relevant than the basic movement programme. The PE programme should be broad enough to include, where possible, recreational activities which may be enjoyed alongside able-bodied pupils. Outdoor pursuits and specialised fitness sessions become appropriate. These may sometimes include carefully chosen weight and circuit training, although it should be noted that general weight training for children is not recommended. Pupils at this stage should also be introduced to a range of options allowing for individual preference. At a senior level pupils can act as

games captains and contribute to the organisation of sports by helping the younger children and setting an example of good practice. Extra-curricular activities and after-school clubs give ideal opportunities for competitive and social experiences, and any chances for special-needs children to participate in sport at local, regional or national level should not be missed.

1.3 Reasons for early movement deprivation

The special-needs child undergoes deprivation of good early movement experience for a variety of reasons:

- the parents may be over-protective: the child is denied the opportunity to explore the environment

- lack of mobility: the world of a chairbound child can be very small

- the child may have been excluded from playing with other children

- schooling may have been sporadic, owing to periods of hospitalisation

- lack of good treatment at an early age

This all adds up to a need for *more* rather than *less* physical activity.

Planners will have to understand normal movement patterns of growth and development, and recognise the need for good early movement training. They should also be aware of the valuable contribution which physical education makes to psychological, emotional and social development. Participation in sports and physical activities helps handicapped children to integrate into the community as active, respected and equal citizens.

1.4 Teachers' problems

Teachers of physical education often have to teach a wide range of pupils in the same class, which makes for difficulties when trying to organise activities suitable for every pupil. These teachers may need to be encouraged to go beyond the traditional approach in which individuals are less important than the class. The practical constraints imposed by having to control thirty children at a time can make it difficult to do the best for individual children, especially those with special needs.

The personal attributes needed to succeed with integrated classes are open attitudes, a determination to overcome difficulties, and the ability to be innovative. There is also the need to remain aware of the realities of the environment and the available facilities. A closed mind will inevitably fail, an open mind will finally find ways of succeeding!

In order to meet the new commitment of integrating children with special needs into the 'main stream', many teachers are now facing the task of looking carefully at methods which they have used successfully for many years.

Often the teachers and their new pupils will be able to cope successfully and safely with the new challenges. However, when adapting to the challenges of teaching children with special needs, there will still be many occasions that will call for great awareness and skill on the part of the teacher.

It is important to be realistic when assessing possible areas of integration with mainstream pupils. In many cases the most suitable answer is for only minor changes to be made to the existing curriculum; a special-needs pupil should not cause the whole curriculum to change. A balance needs to be struck between total integration, which may be impossible, and total segregation, which is at times necessary.

It is crucial to find out as many details about the disabled pupil as possible, and to keep in touch with any later developments. The child's medical adviser should be contacted before physical activities are started. Ideally the medical adviser should receive detailed lists of the proposed activities in which the child will be participating, so that there can be appropriate advice and comment.

1.5 Summary

Planning a programme which includes a handicapped child or children may not be easy, and will depend on a number of criteria. Physical activities must never aggravate any existing condition, and medical opinion should be sought from the outset; activities undertaken should in all instances be complementary to the function of physiotherapy. Each child's limitations should be assessed before choosing an activity, and uppermost in one's mind should be the child's *ability* rather than *disability*. Work and activities in which the children are likely to succeed should be selected. An awareness of hidden handicaps is essential.

Lessons should be organised at both individual and group level, and should include some activities of a recreational flavour. First and foremost, the children should be encouraged to be *participants*, even if for some this has to mean participating as knowledgeable spectators or perhaps as confident officials.

Schools should recognise that there are very few physical activities that a handicapped child cannot take some part in. Disability is only a handicap when opportunity and access are not provided.

Chapter Two
School Policy

The response of a school to requests for integrated physical education can only be achieved after extensive discussion, when all the facts will be known to every teacher involved. In primary education this normally involves whole-staff discussion, while in secondary education a policy could be prepared by the physical education department. This may then need further elaboration and ratification by a curriculum committee or pastoral committee, according to the school's internal organisation.

Parents should be kept fully informed about the proposals for their children's physical education. Parents of non-handicapped pupils need to be similarly aware of the school's physical education philosophy concerning special-needs practices.

Total commitment by all teachers involved is essential if the aims of integrated physical education are to be achieved. However, integration should not be excluded because of the lack of commitment or understanding by unsympathetic members of staff. R. Burns, in his book *Self Concept Development and Education* (1982), explains that teachers are often more sympathetic to children with temporary handicaps than to those with permanent or uncontrollable handicaps:

> These teachers perceive the handicap rather than the child. Such a perceptual block can blind teachers to behavioural clues which in normal circumstances would guide their responses. Teachers' behaviours that tell children that they are not nice to be near or to hear or to see, reflect a negative image of those children's bodily selves.[1]

In-service training may be necessary for certain teachers, to ensure that the scheme does not fail because of them.

2.1 The Physical Education Statement

For some considerable time yet, children will be transferred from existing special schools into mainstream education. It is essential that a *Physical Education Statement* is included within the Main Statement which has to be produced by the special school prior to the child's transfer.

---

[1] This quotation was also used by Jillian Allonby in her paper 'Strategies for developing learning through physical play for children with special educational needs' in 1985 at the 28th International Council for Health, Physical Education and Recreation World Congress.

Currently, many LEAs do not include a section on physical education needs in their statements. School physical educationists, through their head teachers, will need to exert pressure to ensure that their LEA does include such a section.

The composition of such a statement needs very careful preparation if its full value is to be achieved. It should be drawn up by teachers who are knowledgeable not only about physical education in the special-school environment, but who also have expertise in mainstream physical education.

In order for the total spectrum of needs to be assessed, it is essential that the PE departments in secondary schools have access to the whole statement, and not just to those sections that deal specifically with physical education.

The aim of the statement is to ensure that the child's physical education programme in the ordinary school is no less enjoyable, efficient or effective than that received in the special school.

The group composing the statement should address themselves to such areas as those discussed in the remainder of this chapter.

2.2 Communication

Communication with parents

● Parents must be aware of the school policy and what is going to occur

● Parents may need to see active physical education lessons to allay their fears for their children

● Parents should be requested to inform schools of any comments from qualified medical personnel about appropriate or inappropriate activities

Communication with school governors

● Governing bodies need to know proposals for parental consultation and developments in physical education

Communication with local support agencies

● Contact should be be made with appropriate groups, such as charity organisations

Communication with LEA advisory services

● Communication is vital to ensure relevant training for teachers and the supply of appropriate apparatus and resources related to special needs

2.3 General factors
General factors to be covered in the Statement should include:

● nature of the disability

● effects of the disability

● aids needed for mobility

● transport implications

● access to special facilities and movement throughout the school: this should also cover special requirements such as special floor surfaces needed, toileting and showering implications, and waste-disposal problems

● methods of handling

● level of dependency in: dressing, transfer from chair to floor, fitting of aids, feeding

● additional help

● dependence on non-teaching assistants

● links with paramedics

Some of these headings will have been covered in the Main Statement, but it is of considerable advantage if they are repeated with particular reference to physical education.

2.4 The programme
In order to arrive at a well balanced curriculum statement it is helpful to cover the following areas:

● aspects of physical education to be taught

● activities within those disciplines

● levels of achievement

● learning difficulties associated with the disability

● timetable considerations

● frequency of activity

● span of concentration

● teaching methods used

● multi-disciplinary approaches

2.5 Values, attitudes and relationships

In a physical education programme children should be exposed to experiences which develop the following qualities:

● sociability

● confidence

● reliability

● personality

● motivation

● assertiveness

● resilience

2.6 Individual physical development

Attention should be focused on:

● coordination

● agility

● balance

● mobility, strength and power

● capacity to sustain effort

Special-needs teaching can only be properly integrated into mainstream education if full attention is given to groundwork and teamwork.

Chapter Three
Sport and Leisure Activities

This chapter covers a variety of physical activities, both traditional and non-traditional, which can be included in a physical education curriculum. Much emphasis is laid on the specific development of and training for safety, mobility, dexterity and independence. However, no subject is taught in isolation; selection of a subject area is governed by the pupils' needs and the function the course serves, so that mastery of it achieves a meaningful goal. The physical education programme should not be seen in isolation, and natural integration with other curriculum areas should occur at all ages whenever possible.

3.1 Gymnastics

Gymnastics is one of the curriculum activities into which special-needs children may be most easily and totally integrated. It is possible for disabled and able-bodied pupils to work together in pairs and in groups; teachers should be aware of the disadvantages of disabled pupils working together too frequently.

Through the medium of gymnastics, physical skills such as balance, coordination and locomotion can be improved and extended. Body awareness, spatial awareness, timing and rhythm may also be developed and enhanced. Music can also be helpful and beneficial in gymnastics.

Pupils should be encouraged to describe their movements verbally. The use of language is important, although teachers should match their expectations to each pupil's ability.

The British Amateur Gymnastics Association is developing a coaching award to help teachers and coaches who work with special-needs pupils.

3.2 Dance

Dance and creative movement are of considerable value to children with special educational needs. They provide a supporting link with other learning areas, including language, mathematics, the humanities and environmental studies, as well as the creative arts.

Integrating the physical side of learning with the intellectual, imaginative and creative aspects is particularly beneficial for children with special difficulties, who benefit from broad-based approaches to movement and creativity. Through dance they can learn about compensatory alternatives.

In dance it is possible for children to be integrated into the class despite significant individual differences, to move together and yet express their differences satisfactorily. Children who are not readily motivated by the competitive element in some aspects of physical education may gain interest and confidence through dance-related activities.

Body image and body skills are enhanced by positive dance experiences. Coordination is helped by rhythmic activities. Harmonious interaction with the environment is increased by imaginative movement, and social unity is strengthened by the act of dancing with others.

The growth of interest in dance in the community at large, and its inclusion in therapy and fitness programmes, makes it clear that dance should not be omitted from physical education programmes, but should take a prominent place in the physical education curriculum for all children, including those with special educational needs.

3.3 Games

Games are part of our cultural heritage and social structure, and are enjoyed by a large proportion of the population.

Children on the whole love games, and the disabled child is no exception. The guidance teachers give should provide them all with a good foundation for organised games later on.

Teachers need to recognise that major games have evolved as adult pastimes with complex skills and rules. By their very nature, they require a level of technical expertise which young children cannot always be expected to reach, whether handicapped or not. If they are to be enjoyed by children, games must be modified at the learning stage so that they are within the children's capacities. The range of skills and depth of maturity required should match the developmental readiness of the child, both psychologically and physically.

Programmes should be based on the knowledge that the acquisition of skill has no sharp cut-off points, and that linear teaching methods should be adopted. The programme should lead the child through a carefully planned set of progressive experiences, taking account of developmental rather than chronological age. For this linear idea to be pursued successfully it should ideally span both primary and secondary levels, and be divided into a series of progressive stages.

Games may be placed into categories. A popular grouping system is to divide them into *running or invasion, over the net*, and *hitting and fielding* games. One of the many values of using this particular classification is that the common factors or principles within each group are clear. This ensures that a game is not viewed in isolation.

Running or invasion games
This group contains the greatest variety of games, and includes basketball, hockey, netball, soccer, rugby and lacrosse. All the basic skills are employed, and a wide range of body movements used, with the stress on running. Teams are engaged in gaining possession of an object, sending it away and travelling with it, with a view to aiming at a target to score. Opposing teams have equal numbers and share the same territory. Games in the *running or invasion* group may present some difficulty in integrating children with certain types of special needs.

Over the net games
This is a less varied group, consisting of games where a projectile is passed over a net; it includes badminton, tennis, volleyball, batinton, short tennis and quoits. The stress is placed on striking an object with a view to placing it within a defined space on the floor on the opponent's side of the net. This is a more appropriate group for integrating children with special needs.

Hitting and fielding games
This group includes cricket, rounders, softball, baseball and stoolball. The teams operate in a semi-shared space; one group is involved in striking and scoring runs while the other bowls and fields to prevent scoring. Integration is possible but amendments to rules are necessary.

An awareness of these divisions is very helpful in planning a long-term developmental programme.

3.4 Swimming and water activities
This range of physical activities gives good opportunities for all children to realise their potential and to gain a positive attitude towards physical activity. The programme should be carefully structured: the pupils should start by gaining an understanding and use of their own natural buoyancy, and should develop their swimming skills later. At the same time each child should be made aware of the dangers of water and learn simple rescue skills.

All children should be able to understand and practise survival techniques, so that they can participate in water sports such as canoeing, sailing and surf-boarding with safety and confidence. Swimming is one of the areas where fully integrated lessons should be possible. There are many opportunities for cultivating cooperation between pupils with special needs and their able-bodied classmates.

Music and musical activities in the water can be beneficial to all pupils, and may be especially helpful for those with coordination difficulties.

To enable a special-needs child to attend swimming lessons with his/her class, it may be necessary to make some special arrangements. These will depend on the type of handicap or disability, and may involve the following:

- special transport, eg for wheelchairs
- extra help in transporting and changing the child
- extra help on the bath side, especially getting into and out of the water
- extra eyes on the bath side for safety cover

Once in the water the child should be able to participate with the group to which his/her ability relates.

Artificial aids
Some thought will need to be given to the suitability of various swimming aids for different types of handicap. A variety of aids may have to be introduced.

The main categories of swimming aid are:

- *Flotation aids*
These help the individual child find his/her own buoyancy, eg neck collars, graduated body buoyancy.

- *Teaching aids*
These are things that help children to develop their water confidence. Ropes attached across the bath may be of assistance in moving around the bath; objects to go round, through, under and over are a good idea — some above the surface, others semi-submerged; also objects to carry and pick up, and objects to blow and propel.

- *Floats*
These are used to help with swimming techniques. Special-needs children may require floats which are larger than normal or which have some adaptations for them to hold onto easily.

- *Water play aids*
For example, balls with bells inside for blind children, or coloured markers above the water surface for deaf children.

Personal survival techniques
These should be taught as part of a normal lesson. Simple techniques are basically the same for all children, but may have to be adapted. They include:

- how to get out of the water
- how to walk in water
- how to float or find a 'safe position'
- how to stand up from prone and supine positions in the water

All these techniques can be practised as part of the normal lesson.

In all water situations, every child must be aware of emergency drill procedures, and must practise them regularly. Special arrangements for this may have to be made for certain children, such as those with hearing impairments.

Swimming awards
Awards provide a valuable means of motivating all children, including those with special needs. It is important that these children should have tangible goals. The choice of award to be aimed at will be the responsibility of the teacher. There are many national awards to be considered, including those of the ASA, ESSA, STA, RLSS, SASA and SSSA. Some awards are designed especially for the handicapped, including those of the ASA/ESSA and of the SASA/SSSA.

3.5 Athletics and cross-country
As can be seen from the wide range of athletic events organised for all disability groups from local to international level, this area of the curriculum is in no way closed to the child with special needs. As many events are of an individual nature, day-to-day lessons need not be disrupted by the presence of a handicapped child if they are carefully planned.

Track
A chairbound child can work with the rest of the group so long as the ground is dry and firm and the grass close-cut; allowances for pace and distance must be made. If there is more than one chairbound child in the group, they can work together alongside the rest of the group, joining in where appropriate. Relays are a good and popular way of encouraging integration.

It is interesting to note that racing wheelchairs are now so sophisticated that people without handicaps are taking up wheelchair racing.

Throws
Javelin, discus and shot are events suitable for able-bodied and handicapped alike, so total integration should take place. If a pupil cannot throw a javelin, a rounders or cricket ball can be thrown instead. If the pupil cannot manage a discus, an Indian club can be substituted. Throwing the Indian club is a recognised event for the disabled. Investment in an Indian club and a short, 400-gram javelin may be considered worthwhile. Many activities can be designed around target areas rather than simply throwing for distance.

Jumps
Depending on the handicap and on medical advice, it may be possible for jumping to be attempted. If jumping is not possible, the child can still remain a part of the group, actively and usefully employed in measuring and recording.

Cross-country
It will be impossible for some disabled pupils to manage cross-country running as it is generally understood. However, it is often possible to devise special routes in and around the school using different levels: along corridors, through doors, and up, down and over ramps.

Potted sports
These are very valuable for all children.

Useful additional material concerning athletics for the handicapped is provided by:

● The British Sports Association for the Disabled (BSAD), which has a coaching scheme plus information on classification (beyond school level in particular)

● Ten Step Award Scheme

● Amateur Athletics Association: *Fun Athletics*

3.6 Outdoor education and adventure activities
Outdoor education is a term used to cover educational activities concerned with living, moving and learning in the outdoor environment. Thus outdoor activities combine physical outdoor pursuits with study of the environment. The two aspects are closely interrelated, to the extent that one can hardly participate in outdoor pursuits *without* learning about the environment.

Outdoor pursuits
Some children with special needs are not motivated towards participation in highly structured or competitive activities. Such children may benefit from an introduction to one or more of a wide range of outdoor pursuits: camping, hill-walking, rock climbing, orienteering, caving, canoeing, sailing etc. In such activities the emphasis is on enjoyable participation and personal satisfaction rather than on overt competition and the achievement of elite standards. A great deal of help and guidance can be obtained from the national governing bodies of these sports.

It must be borne in mind that not all outdoor pursuits are appropriate for all children with special needs. Great care must be taken by the teacher in choosing the right activity for each child. The teacher should emphasise the child's abilities rather than disabilities, seeking those activities in which the child can participate and realise his/her full potential.

It may be necessary to adapt equipment or purchase different equipment. For example, slalom canoes with narrow cockpits are not suitable for some handicapped children because of the difficulty of getting out in the event of a capsize. In such cases, a two-man canoe would be better.

Great thought should be given to the venue for the activity. For example, children in wheelchairs have a restricted field of vision, yet in order to take their bearings they must be able to see the features of a place. Similarly, access to canoes and sailing dinghies can pose problems for children who cannot walk or who are only partly ambulant.

Many physically handicapped children become cold very quickly, and must be well protected from the elements. Such children usually have to work harder at a task than able-bodied children, and are more likely to suffer from exhaustion or exposure. It is important to have a 'buddy system' whereby an able-bodied child works closely with a child with special needs — not to do everything for him/her, but to be there to offer assistance if and when required.

Environmental studies
In environmental studies, the 'buddy system' can again be used to good effect, with the able-bodied collecting specimens and taking them to their partners for joint identification.

Some children with special needs may require separate worksheets with less difficult language and simpler tasks.

As much preparation as possible should be done indoors to minimise waiting about outside if the weather is inclement.

Again, much thought should be given to venues: will the non-ambulant or partly ambulant children be able to get to the sites?

Teaching outdoor education to mixed groups puts tremendous demands on teachers in terms of preparation and organisation. However, it remains an excellent vehicle for integration: children with special needs and the able-bodied can gain a deeper understanding of each other through their enjoyment and satisfaction in working together.

3.7 Recreational activities
There is another large group of less energetic but greatly rewarding and pleasurable pursuits which schools should encourage among their pupils: this group includes games such as darts, billiards, table tennis, carpet bowls, and other activities such as wheelchair dancing, obstacle courses and spontaneous rhythmic dancing.

By using thought and imagination, many simple activities matching pupils' needs and abilities can be found. It is often within the capacity of the pupils to devise their own games or to adapt existing activities to their own needs. The Duke of Edinburgh's Award scheme can be of some support in broadening the scope of the school's PE programme.

3.8 Health-focused physical education for secondary pupils with special needs

A personal health focus should be part of every physical education lesson. In this way all pupils will have the chance to discover their own strength, suppleness and stamina while participating in athletics, dance, games, gymnastics and swimming. A pupil-centred approach allows all pupils to be more easily integrated into the class, as well as enabling them to monitor their own achievement and progress.

If the activity programme during the first two years of secondary schooling is well balanced in this way, it will enhance physical and personal skill development, encouraging the pupils to take part in individual, pair and group situations.

A programme concentrating on more specific aspects of health can then be introduced for the senior students, providing them with appropriate equipment to challenge and test their personal physical condition. Checks can be made on flexibility, cardio-vascular fitness, etc. Individual students can devise programmes aimed at improving their own performances. Together with their peers and teachers they can work towards establishing realistic targets.

● personally focused activities give a strong impetus to self-motivation

● recording achievement provides a useful database and reflects the true value of regular exercise

● studying nutrition and how to lead a healthy lifestyle completes the health focus

Students who follow such a programme should become well-motivated individuals who know themselves and are capable of making informed decisions which will benefit their whole lives.

3.9 Knowledge-based physical education

The aim of becoming a 'knowledgeable spectator' may be considered thoroughly worthwhile for pupils who are unable to participate fully in the physical education programme. To do so, these pupils must develop the competence to examine the actions of others and to make informed judgements about professional and non-professional performances in dance, drama, gymnastics and various aspects of sport.

This means that the physical education programme needs to:

● give opportunities for pupils to gain an understanding of the principles of movement

● enable pupils to appreciate standards of performance, recognise shortcomings, and be able to suggest how to apply movement principles to overcome them

● enable pupils to recognise individual variations in movement aptitude

● give pupils an understanding of the value of each individual activity in the physical education curriculum and also of extra-curricular activities

● allow pupils to judge the physical mastery of skills and techniques, and understand the rules, conventions and tactics of each game

To achieve this, teachers can make use of a wide variety of media, including various audio-visual techniques and carefully prepared videos and films. Current sporting events can be followed, developing the pupils' ability to be informed spectators.

Having a positive role in some parts of the physical education curriculum should enable the special-needs pupil to consider critically the nature of many kinds of physical activity. Practical involvement and participation in refereeing, scoring and judging will provide opportunities for enriching the pupil's ability to interpret and respond to what is observed.

Chapter Four
Teaching Methodology

Teaching strategies and methods of coaching are well documented and therefore readily accessible. However, selecting the most appropriate of these to match children's individual needs and abilities requires careful deliberation. The teachers must have specific knowledge about both the child and the activity, and be aware of critical factors such as time allocation, facilities available, number of helpers etc.

4.1 Adapting facilities and equipment

For the majority of children with special needs, the content of the programme, the way it is taught and the facilities and equipment used, need not differ greatly from the norm. However, where adaptations are necessary, teachers may need some guidance. Discussion with colleagues is perhaps the richest source of inspiration, as there is a wealth of knowledge in this area which is hitherto untapped and unrecorded. Publications such as the Kent and Lancashire LEA booklets give documented examples and are worth reading.

If a ball game is the selected activity with a group of partially sighted children, then the size of the object and its colour would be selected as being of prime consideration; the teacher may decide that providing a luminous coloured object of a particular texture is most appropriate.

Teachers may find it necessary to make modifications in one or more of the following main areas:

● facilities

● the rules

● the activity

● equipment

Here are some typical examples:

● Contain ball games in enclosed spaces, thus reducing the problem of the ball always going out of control

● Change the size of the work space, thus reducing or increasing the distance for either a pupil or an object to travel

● Cover the work area with mats so that wheelchair users can play at floor level safely when out of their chairs

● Vary the size, texture, weight, length or height of equipment used

- Use foam balls, which are light and can be held in one hand
- Use low-density balls which have a slow bounce and are therefore easier to control
- Try using a balloon or a beach ball in a game of volleyball, as it tends to stay in the air for a longer period of time, giving the pupils more chance to see it
- Using tethered balls will ensure continuity of action
- Lightweight bats and rackets, and those with short handles, are particularly useful for one-handed players
- Mobility aids can be used very profitably in games sessions, eg chariots and trolleys
- Use 'bleeper' balls or those containing bells or ball bearings for children who have visual difficulties
- Keep a good supply of replacements for projectiles which cannot be retrieved quickly, eg table-tennis balls, bean bags etc
- Use gadgets to help children retrieve objects easily from the floor, eg a tube or a fishing net to collect table-tennis balls
- Keep activities simple to start with, and then progress. Remember, the easiest ball to hit is large and stationary; it becomes more difficult when balls are smaller and when they are rolled, bounced or thrown
- Games such as handball and rounders can be integrated by making adjustments to the rules. In handball, a wheelchair user can be a goalkeeper if seated on a mat in front of the goal; in Danish rounders, the fielders could be required to throw the ball round the square twice when a disabled pupil is batting. In field rounders the disabled pupil can use a larger bat, with the backstop not being permitted to throw the ball to first base.

Awareness and consideration of these factors when planning programmes should help the children to achieve a feeling of success which will surely result in increased satisfaction, greater enjoyment and overall improvement.

4.2 Summary

Education is concerned with offering experiences to pupils to improve the quality of their lives.

The concept of excellence for the individual needs to be considered. Teachers need to strive to achieve excellence and to give of their best, often in uncongenial circumstances. Likewise, severely disabled children may within their limitations achieve an excellence of effort and skill. Both teacher and pupil need a discerning eye and knowledge to see and appreciate this.

Because each child is a unique individual, and because so often handicaps are multiple, one can only give examples of possible solutions and strategies. These suggestions have been included to provide some help and to encourage teachers to be creative and innovative in their attitudes to problems. Any thoughts are better than none, and one can start from this premise and find solutions to many problems. One needs to be an idealist as well as a realist, and to hold on to the possibility of miracles despite the limitations of the environment and of individual energy. Miracles can be made to happen!

Chapter Five
Safety

In order to meet the new commitment of integrating children with special needs into the 'mainstream', many teachers are now facing the task of looking more carefully at the way they teach, even though they may have been successful for many years.

5.1 Safety and good practice

Often teachers and the new pupils will be able to cope successfully and safely with the new challenges, but there will be many occasions when adaptation of the task to meet the hindered responses of special-needs children will call for great awareness and skill. These points should be borne in mind:

● The child is relying on the teacher to set work with which he/she can cope while trying to improve performance

● Parents are even more reliant on the teacher's skill and judgement to get the task right. The teacher has a higher duty of care, and is expected to follow good practice

● Consideration must be given to the environment in which the child is working, as it might prove hostile to the pupil's limited ability

● There is a need to create a supportive atmosphere among all the other pupils which encourages and cares without impeding their 'special' colleagues or their own progress

● Everybody needs to know a lot about safe practice and to be able to apply it confidently and progressively

● When adapting any apparatus, care must be taken not to reduce its stability

● Teachers must take particular care if improvised adaptations are made to furniture, such as chairs or benches. There must be absolutely no risk of slippage, rocking or collapse. Working space needs careful thought

● Some of the children may suffer a sharp deterioration of performance level. Teachers must watch for the onset of fatigue and help children to identify this problem in themselves

● Children in wheelchairs need space in which to move, and a well maintained and properly designed chair in which to sit. Those around whom the chairs move need to be constantly alert

● There must be a well managed system of first aid

Teachers should ask themselves: 'What would I feel like if my child were being placed in this position?' If the teacher has any doubt, then it would be better not to allow the activity to continue. The teacher is *protector* as well as *provider*, and must try to foresee the outcomes of anything which is asked of pupils, especially of those who do not learn easily. The implications of the foregoing ten points can be focused into the following three sections.

5.2 Safety strategy for teachers

By forward planning, all teachers should equip themselves with a working strategy in which safety is paramount. In particular, the head of the physical education department must see that there is an active safety policy in being and that all teachers are knowledgeable operatives of the scheme. New members joining the staff will need inducting into the scheme. There are several books listed in the bibliography (Chapter 10.1) which give practical advice on safety matters.

Care should be taken to find out what the employing authority's policy on safety is. They may have very specific regulations and bye-laws, and teachers must be aware of these. Many authorities provide their own notes for guidance on safety in physical education, and these must be incorporated into the working practices of the school.

In activities where speed of movement and time management are critical, the scheme of work must show awareness of the need and a reasonable resolution of the problem so far as special-needs pupils are involved. For example, if these children are asked to attempt a gymnastic activity involving height, flight and any transfer of body weight, the time allocated to execute the manoeuvre must be reasonable. The risk of failure must be avoided by the provision of manual support or soft material.

The learning difficulties experienced by special-needs pupils will vary considerably in type and degree. What a 'safe' teacher will need to show is that the work attempted is adapted to each child so that there is a high expectation of safe accomplishment. This means that the system within the school must give a clear picture of each pupil's needs, and develop a realistic programme to match them.

Motor control will pose special problems so far as safety is concerned. Special-needs children should not be exposed abruptly to the practice of skills in which success requires precise motor control. Very simple breakdown of the total pattern of execution will ease the difficulty, enhance the chance of learning and, above all, improve safety. Teachers who have developed a good attitude to safety will recognise that frequent repetition of the exercise helps consolidation of the skill being learned. They will also be aware that progress is often represented by the acquisition of the most minute degree of improvement. A safe child is one who knows that such minute achievement is recognised, and that it is not necessary to over-reach one's ability in order to impress the teacher.

5.3 The environment

Much advice has already been given by the Department of Education and Science and by BAALPE concerning a safe working environment for physical education in schools. This needs expanding to cover the integration of 'special-needs learning'.

Pupils with limited mobility will need help with their circulation around the school: easy entry into the physical education areas, especially changing rooms, showers and playing fields, will need to be provided. This may require extra support and awareness from all able-bodied pupils. A safe scheme will take this into account. The normal practices of tidy storage rooms, properly accessible equipment, good door management and the posting of warning notices and advice may need further adaptation for hindered pupils: for example, notice boards may need to be much lower for wheelchair pupils; to help those whose reading skills are poor, essential safety notices may be more effective as pictorial messages rather than as written instructions.

Perhaps the most helpful part of any safety scheme will be the development of the normal pupils' awareness and involvement so that they will exercise good levels of support to ease and strengthen the integration of their peers.

Chapter Six

Assessment

The physical education curriculum of special-needs pupils should provide a highly personalised programme. To ensure that there is adequate progression during the teaching of the programme, careful monitoring of skills, concerning physical development and body management as well as attitudes and sociability, is necessary.

6.1 General organisation

Any system of assessment should be based on the teaching programme, not the reverse! This will ensure that the child receives a rounded physical education, and that the minimum amount of time is spent on testing procedures.

The results of the monitoring and assessment will need to be recorded on cards. These will be of benefit to the teaching, medical and paramedical staff, and to the children's parents. As well as recording progress, the cards should aim to motivate the children and maintain their interest in physical education.

There are some excellent assessment models available. Some of these are on the commercial market, while others have been devised by special schools for their own use. Contact should be made with the local special schools to determine the system in use. Where there are both physically and mentally handicapped pupils, it may be necessary to develop two systems of recording in order to reflect the different special needs and aptitudes of these groups.

It is an advantage if a 'cluster' of schools, using their special schools as 'centres of excellence', devise a system of assessment and recording that is common across the cluster.

Wherever possible, the assessment and recording should be carried out by the children themselves, or by a 'buddy' if the partner system is in use, thus ensuring that the children are aware of their own progress. This will involve the staff of the physical education department in a commitment to child-based assessment in their general teaching role.

To ensure that the children's interest is maintained, it is essential that the steps of progression to be assessed are kept small. In this way success is seen to be achieved on a regular basis, and it becomes an effective additional aid to motivation.

It must be recognised that the essential commitment to assessment and recording will involve certain changes within the management system of the physical education department in the secondary school. In the primary school there will probably be an increase in the work-load and responsibilities of the curriculum leader.

To set up a really effective assessment and recording system, it will be necessary to discuss and decide on a strategy covering management, assessment, monitoring of pupil feedback, recording method, development of pupil profiles, and unit accreditation. These essential components are now considered separately:

6.2 Management
The following points must be addressed:

● What are the aims and objectives of the assessment and recording system?

● What outside influences may affect the system:
   ○ school profiling?
   ○ medical and paramedical staff?
   ○ examination schedules?
   ○ governing bodies of sport?

● How will the special-needs assignment and recording fit into the existing departmental procedure?

● Which units of work are to be assessed?

● How will these units be prepared — according to method, form, staff or expertise?

● What are the sources of finance for:
   ○ testing equipment?
   ○ recording?

● Just what sort of data storage systems should be used? Which method of filing and system of retrieval?

● What place will pupil feedback have in the assessment process?

● What training in reciprocal and experiential learning will be given to children to aid pupil feedback?

● What INSET training is necessary to ensure that all members of staff perform adequately in the assessment process?

6.3 Assessment categories

● What types and categories of assessment are to be used?

● How often will assessment be carried out:
   ○ continuous?
   ○ each week?
   ○ after each unit of work?
   ○ each term?

- Who will carry out the assessment:
  - the staff?
  - the children?
  - the paramedical assistants?
  - the parents?
  - a combination of these?

- How will the criteria of assessment be kept constant between staff members?

- What type of grading system will be used?

- Where does criteria referencing fit into the scheme?
- Will the scheme rely only on subjective assessment, or will objective tests be used?

6.4 Pupil feedback

It is essential that a process of continual pupil feedback is built into the physical education programme.

The majority of teachers have never experienced the problems of skill learning encountered by the handicapped. By movement observation, and in particular by pupil feedback, teachers can come to appreciate the problems and thus be in a position to assist the learning processes.

Good feedback will enable the teacher to:

- ensure that the children have understood the set task

- develop the children's skill in observing and commenting on movement

- ascertain what the children believe they have learned

- involve the children in a process of written self- assessment

To achieve these objectives the teacher will need to employ various teaching methods during the lesson. It may be necessary to use one of a variety of questionnaires after a lesson, group of lessons, or module has been taught.

Much has been written about this type of approach both in education in general and in physical education in particular. Staff will need to determine which models fit their specific needs.

It cannot be emphasised enough that pupil feedback is of the utmost importance in the field of special need.

6.5 Documentation

A review should be made of the style of recording used in the school. Can the existing record cards be used, or do they need to be adapted? Does a completely new type of card need to be designed? If so, how will this affect the existing system?

The following check-list will aid the review and also assist with the design of a new card, if necessary. Remember — you are assessing and recording ability, not disability!

● Is the title of the record clear?

● Is the pupil's name prominently placed?

● Is there a space for the pupil's photograph?

● Are contact points for parents and doctors included?

● Are prohibited activities clearly stated and displayed?

● Is the layout easy to follow, with clear printing, unambiguous wording and a key for decoding any abbreviations?

● Is the card of a manageable size for storage, clarity and ease of completion?

● Are there adequate spaces for additional comments, dates and times of entries, and for parents' comments?

● Is the content of the card relevant to the aims and objectives of your assessment process?

● Does the card indicate the criteria used for assessment?

● Is extra work required to send a copy to parents?

6.6 Pupil profiles

Profiles are documents constructed by professional teachers describing as accurately and succinctly as possible the knowledge, skills and experience of an individual relative to a particular curriculum.

Further Education Unit, Department of Education and Science, 1982

Records of Achievement: A Statement of Policy, a DES document published in 1984, states:

The Secretaries of State hope that it will be possible by the end of the decade to establish throughout England and Wales arrangements under which all young people in secondary schools will have records of achievement and will take with them when they leave school a summary document of record prepared within a framework of national policy which leaves scope for local variations.

If special-needs pupils in mainstream education are to receive the many benefits a well-devised profile can bestow on them, then careful attention needs to be paid to the aims and objectives of such profiles.

The Statement of Policy quoted above states that there are four main purposes of profiles. These should be borne in mind whenever recording systems are under discussion.

1 Recognition of achievement
Records and recording systems should recognise, acknowledge and give credit for what pupils have achieved and experienced, not just in terms of results in public examinations, but in other ways as well. They should do justice to pupils' own efforts and to the efforts of teachers, parents, ratepayers and taxpayers to give them a good education.

2 Motivation and personal development
Records should contribute to pupils' personal development and progress by improving their motivation, providing encouragement and increasing their awareness of strengths, weaknesses and opportunities.

3 Curriculum and organisation
The recording process should help schools to identify the all-round potential of their pupils and to consider how well their curriculum, teaching and organisation enable pupils to develop the general, practical and social skills which are to be recorded.

4 A document of record
Young people leaving school or college should take with them a summary document of record which is recognised and valued by employers and institutions of further and higher education. This should provide a more rounded picture of candidates for jobs or courses than can be provided by a list of examination results, thus helping potential users to decide how candidates could best be employed, or for which jobs, training schemes or courses they are likely to be suitable.

The profile should concentrate on positive aspects; it should show personal achievements and characteristics, with evidence of attainment in both academic and practical skills.

Teachers should allow the children to see their own profiles: each one is a child's personal record, and he or she should be given access to it.

The major problem in physical education with special-needs pupils is national accreditation of academic ability linked to skill.

There are many excellent graded tests in aspects of physical education for the handicapped, and full use should be made of these for pupil motivation and accreditation. (See national governing bodies' handbooks for examples.)

6.7 Unit accreditation

For national accreditation of academic attainment linked to practical skills it is recommended that schools should examine the *Unit Accreditation Scheme* run by the various examination boards in the country.

The *Statement of Achievement System*, organised by the examination boards, has much to offer teachers of special-needs pupils who wish to include nationally accredited work in a pupil's profile.

The criteria of a unit complement the individual programme of the special-needs pupil. This is because each unit:

● reflects the potential of the pupils

● is a short module of work and therefore has short-term goals

● is about the attaining of targets

● indicates frequent recognition of achievement

● is taken when pupils are ready

● is criterion-referenced

● is about the process rather than the product

● has pupil involvement at all stages

As the unit of work is determined by the school, it can be linked directly to the abilities, aptitudes and needs of the pupils. The unit can include life skills as well as the practical skills included in normal examinations.

These points make the scheme of particular benefit because national accreditation can be given to those types of skills which could aid children with special needs in their bid for employment.

6.8 Building a unit

An example of a unit, in this case one specially devised for children in wheelchairs, could include some of the following areas of work:

Wheelchair proficiency

● Mobility
  ○ forward and backward movement with left and right turns
  ○ moving into rooms — opening and closing doors
  ○ slalom course skill
  ○ 'wheelie'
  ○ transfer from wheelchair to floor and return

- Maintenance
  - remove and replace wheelchair arm
  - inflate and instruct how to inflate tyre
  - check brakes, footrest and seat belt
  - repair a puncture

- Road sense
  - show a working knowledge of the Green Cross Code
  - show awareness of danger to non-wheelchair users
  - instruct a person how to manoeuvre a chair up and down a kerb
  - demonstrate a knowledge of safe places to cross a road

- Academic. Demonstrate knowledge of:
  - the history of the wheel
  - the design of wheelchairs
  - the theory of levers
  - the wheel and power

- Athletic skills. Participate in:
  - track events
  - field events
  - invasion games
  - aiming games
  - table tennis
  - slalom courses

Once the academic and movement capabilities of the child are known, appropriate items may be extracted from the list to construct a worthwhile unit.

Chapter Seven

Practical Considerations in the School

Before describing some of the more common handicapping conditions which teachers may encounter, we first consider some of the down-to-earth questions which should be faced if integration is to be successful:

7.1 The children and their personalities

● Have the parents been consulted? Their knowledge of their child and their support is vital.

● Has expert advice been taken? This should be sought from the appropriate GPs, physicians, medical officers, therapists, support teachers, etc.

● Is the medication which a child may be taking known, and are its possible implications understood?

● Are there any special emergency procedures of which teachers should be aware?

● Are the notes on the child up to date? Has any unusual behaviour been recorded?

● Does the child's personality affect his/her ability to cope, or vice versa?

7.2 Equipment and resources

● Will any special resources be needed, such as special equipment for PE lessons?

● Are physical aids involved? Will the teacher and the children have to accommodate sticks, crutches, rollators or wheelchairs? Do any of them wear a brace, calipers or splints, a hearing aid or spectacles? Are such aids in good condition?

● Do any of the children need special protective clothing?

7.3 Practical mobility

● Will help be required for toileting and changing, or during the PE lesson?

● Will privacy have to be arranged for toileting and changing?

● Can special-needs pupils move freely without danger to themselves or the other children?

● Are all the PE spaces accessible to special-needs children — corridors, doorways, changing rooms, showers, toilets, gymnasium, hall, swimming pool, hard play areas, fields?

● Has allowance been made for the extra time which handicapped children need to perform most tasks associated with the PE lesson — getting to and from the PE area, changing and physical activities? Time must be given, and *patience* will be required from all concerned.

● Have the necessary allowances been made for the problems caused by hospitalisation? Pupils suffering from some conditions require frequent absence from school for surgery, therapy or recuperation. It is easy for these children to fall behind with their work. Teachers should take these circumstances into account when planning their re-integration into lessons.

The above list may appear rather daunting, but it is a teacher's professional responsibility to look for ability and to extend potential. A little extra pre-planning and care will be required to ensure that these 'special' children receive the challenging and enjoyable physical education to which they are entitled.

Chapter Eight

Handicapping Conditions and their Implications for Physical Education

This chapter describes the more common conditions which teachers may encounter, and gives guidance on appropriate physical education activities and procedures.

8.1 Arthritis (Still's Disease)

Still's Disease is a progressive disease which in the main affects the joints but sometimes involves other body systems. *Rheumatoid arthritis* causes inflammation of the joints, which become swollen and tender. The surrounding tissues become thickened and restrict mobility. The pain and stiffness vary from day to day, and are most severe early in the morning.

Sometimes inflammation of the eye is associated with arthritis, and this may lead to difficulties with vision.

The condition is treated with drugs and physiotherapy. Normally joints need to be put through their whole range of movement to prevent them becoming fixed.

Some children affected by arthritis have to wear splints on their wrists and ankles.

Physical education implications

● It is essential that advice is sought from parents and the child's physiotherapist before undertaking any physical activity.

● Hands and feet are most commonly affected, so any activity which could cause twisting and jarring to the feet, such as jumping, should always be avoided.

● Gripping can cause problems, for example in the gymnasium or in some games skills.

● Because of stiffness and pain in the joints, the child may require more time for general movement.

● General clumsiness may be evident.

● Swimming is very beneficial as it removes weight-bearing loads.

8.2 Asthma

Asthma is a common condition which narrows or restricts the air passages of the lungs. It occurs in three ways:

● the muscles in the airways contract causing a spasm

● the lining of the airways becomes swollen and irritated

● too much mucus is produced in the lungs

The most noticeable symptoms of asthma are shortness of breath, wheezing and coughing. The severity of attacks varies considerably from mild, which may need no special treatment, to severe attacks which require prompt medical assistance.

Several factors, sometimes in combination, may provoke an attack:

● virus infection

● excessive exercise

● sudden changes in temperature

● allergic reaction to certain foods, drugs, pollen, etc

● excitement and stress

● overtiredness

Physical education implications

● Children with asthma should not be allowed to use their condition as an excuse to avoid physical education. Anxiety sometimes causes a child to adop this attitude. A reluctance to participate should be discussed with parents.

● Because of previous experiences, vigorous exercise and extremes of temperature may cause a child to be anxious about the possibility of an attack during the physical education lesson. A thorough warm-up is essential. Attacks can often be prevented by the child using a bronchiodilator inhaler, and asthmatic children for whom these have been prescribed should be encouraged to carry one with them. One alternative treatment requires the taking of a tablet about twenty minutes before the lesson. The use of appropriate drugs will usually allow asthma sufferers to participate normally. Exhaling should be stressed in the event of an attack.

● Children with asthma may participate in all physical education activities, but care should be taken to avoid prolonged strenuous exercise.

● Swimming in short bursts has been found to be particularly beneficial, but over-heated or under-heated pools should be avoided.

● Children with asthma may need constant encouragement.

8.3 Behavioural deviation

Many children displaying severe behavioural deviance attend day and residential special schools, and derive great benefit from physical education designed to meet their specific needs: mainstream schools are not likely to be able to support such pupils. However, there are certain behaviourally disturbed children who can cope with the corporate school ethos, and given sensitive teaching support and an appropriate physical education programme, they can both benefit from and contribute to it.

Generally, these pupils will present an aggressive stance towards physical education, either by verbal or physical means, or by simply opting out. No progress will be made unless the teacher can establish a negotiating platform and display an understanding of the whole problem. The pupil needs to be treated with proper sympathy and shown an acceptable way forward. It can be helpful if the pupil is able to indicate some previous pleasure, success or skill in physical education.

Many children with severe behavioural problems have a poor self-image and consequently poor self-esteem. The teacher's main task will be to improve the former in order to enhance the latter.

Physical education implications

● A rich motor experience in the formative years, which includes self-expression and some measure of self-determination, will promote a good body-image. Creative dance and drama sensitively handled will do much to encourage a positive self-image and allow for self-expression.

● Some pupils will cope well with team games, but many will have difficulty in coping with peer relationships. In such cases small groups and individual work will often be more successful. The teacher's individual approach to these children in terms of challenges, responses, solutions and successes will help the pupil to develop a more positive self-image and thereby enrich self-esteem.

● Complicated skills teaching may be hostile for these children, as may be sophisticated social relationships. Work broken down to simple skill components with rhythmic learning patterns will be helpful, particularly if there is a successful outcome to each component.

● Swimming, basic trampolining, simple challenge gymnastics, small-group games, stamina-loaded circuit training and controlled strength work are all elements which can make the physical education programme attractive for these children.

8.4 Brittle bones

Brittle bones is usually an inherited condition resulting in an abnormality of the protein structure of the bones which causes them to break more easily than normal. Also the ligaments are often lax and the joints more mobile than is usual. Occasionally a child's hearing may be impaired.

In some children fractures may occur without warning and for no apparent reason, but nevertheless it is important not to overprotect them. All activities should be discussed beforehand with the parents and the physiotherapist.

In more severe cases the children are small and the bones are twisted as a result of frequent fractures. These children can rarely join in class activities physically, but enjoy being judges or umpires. Advice on lifting and handling must be sought from the parents before the child comes into school.

Children with this condition usually require regular physiotherapy. More severely affected children use special wheelchairs for safety and support, and those less severely affected may use sticks or crutches. Most children with brittle bones are severely restricted in mobility. This can often lead to frustration and may affect their attitude to learning. Children who fracture easily may have frequent long stays in hospital and may fall behind with their work.

Physical education implications

● Because of the nature of this condition many forms of physical education are not suitable. However, some exercise is essential for general fitness.

● Swimming is ideal, as are other non-weight-bearing and non-restricted activities.

● Care must be taken in getting in and out of swimming baths and in the general handling of these children.

● Consultation with parents, doctors and physiotherapists must take place before any exercise is undertaken.

● Crowded corridors, changing rooms and playgrounds need to be avoided to minimise the risk of bumping and knocking. Children with brittle bones need to be given space.

8.5 Cardiac conditions and congenital heart disease

These require special attention because of the primary importance of the heart to the child's life.

Generalisations should not be made about heart conditions. The teacher must seek expert advice from the child's parents and physician about the advisability of and degree of participation in physical activity.

Congenital heart disease

This term signifies that a heart defect has been present from birth. In some cases the condition may be very mild and need no treatment. The most common defect is called *hole in the heart*.

A few children who are awaiting surgery, and those whose condition cannot be completely cured, need special consideration, but some may be able to join in certain aspects of the curriculum.

Physical education implications

● Some children with heart disease can lead normal lives and should be allowed to participate in physical education.

● Where heart disease causes circulatory problems, there may be breathlessness and blueness of the lips and nail beds, and the child will tire very quickly.

● Special consideration should be given to the temperature of the water when swimming and to safety aspects and procedures in case a child becomes exhausted in the water.

● Teachers *must* consult parents and receive the correct medical advice about the appropriate level of activity and capabilities of the child.

8.6 Cerebral palsy

There are three main forms of cerebral palsy: *spasticity*, *athetosis* and *ataxia*.

Cerebral palsy is a disorder of movement and posture which is caused by damage to, or lack of development of, the part of the brain controlling movement. Sometimes the damage also causes deafness and other difficulties in perception.

The condition can be classified according to the part of the body involved:

Paraplegia	both legs
Quadriplegia	all four limbs
Diplegia	four limbs but legs more than arms
Hemiplegia	arm and leg on same side of the body

The effects of cerebral palsy vary widely, from slight handicap, such as an unsteady gait, to severe multiple disabilities. These may include sensory impairment, epilepsy and mental handicap. It is unlikely that multiple-handicapped children will attend an ordinary school.

Physical education implications

● Spatial and/or perceptual difficulties are common.

● Some children have poor motor organisation which may affect physical education. For example, ball-handling skills may prove difficult, and careful attention to correct sequencing will be helpful.

● Grasping and releasing is often difficult for the child with this condition. Special balls with a highly textured surface are helpful, and bean bags are easier to catch than balls. Foam balls are also useful.

● Moving objects can be difficult to deal with, and teachers can help by making simple adaptations such as remembering that it is easier to catch a ball which is bounced than one which is thrown. Similarly, the children will find it easier to hit a stationary ball than one which is moving.

● Sudden sharp sounds should be avoided, because they might induce muscle spasm and thus hinder therapeutic work.

● Swimming in warm water can be of great importance to help with relaxation. Usually children suffering from spasticity should be introduced to the water in the 'face upwards' (supine) position. They usually have difficulty in exhaling, and therefore the importance of controlled breathing and reverting to the supine position should be stressed. After swimming, care must be taken to return the child gradually to normal body and air temperature. Severe chilling can induce spasms.

● In any activity the correct starting position is very important, whether lying, standing or sitting.

● Some children may have balancing problems and may be more prone to falling over than other children. This may be overcome by the use of aids such as sticks and rollators which should be checked for wear from time to time. If the rubber ferrules on the tips are worn, the parents should be notified and replacements provided.

● Children with speech and other communication problems will need extra time and patience from the teacher.

● Dressing and undressing for PE may be difficult. As far as possible, allow the pupil time to do this for himself/herself.

● Tiredness may set in more easily for children with an appreciable disability, because they need to use more energy to achieve the same goals.

● Teachers must remember that for some pupils insistent urging to greater effort may be counter-productive because of over-activated motor control. Such pupils may even need relaxation regimes prior to increased muscular effort, but they should not be excluded from any class work.

8.7 Clumsiness

Clumsiness (*minimal motor dysfunction*) is relative. This section is concerned with those children who appear to be clumsy at most things, lacking in coordination of physical movement, and frequently displaying behavioural disorders.

In a minority of cases clumsiness may arise out of such conditions as degenerative diseases, head injuries, deafness and defective vision. However, the perceptual motor disabilities which give rise to most cases of clumsiness are usually acquired at or before birth, and seem to be due largely to minimal brain dysfunction. Medical evidence suggests that defects in the receiving and passing on of messages to and from the brain result in lack of coordination of eyesight and bodily movement, and sometimes cause speech disorders.

There is no typically clumsy child, and the condition is not necessarily related to intelligence. However, some of the most frequently observed behavioural and learning difficulties of those deemed clumsy are listed below:

● hyperactivity and restlessness: always on the go

● perceptual motor impairments: frequent falls, marked inability in some handling skills such as drawing, writing, tying shoe-laces and doing up buttons

● erratic emotional behaviour: unexplained outbursts of behaviour tantrums

● attention disorders: lack of concentration and perseverance

These symptoms may exist in varying degrees and clusters, and it is unlikely that they arise solely from brain dysfunction. More likely, they will be the combined result of frustration, low self-esteem, lack of patience and repeated failure.

It is important that clumsiness is identified early and that all persons dealing with the child understand the problems and work together towards the remedy.

Physical education implications

● A carefully structured all-round physical education programme can make a major contribution to improving the self-esteem and confidence of the clumsy child.

● Individual activities such as gymnastics and creative dance, where children are responding to tasks at their own level of ability, will be helpful. Sensitive handling will be required in competitive situations. Effort and success must be recognised and praise should be constant.

● All work on balance, rhythm and coordination will be helpful. Both gross and fine motor skills will usually require breaking down into the simplest stages of progression.

● Spatial and perceptual difficulties are common.

● Poor motor organisation may be evident. Ball-handling skills may prove difficult, and careful attention to correct sequencing is essential for progress.

● Moving objects may be difficult to deal with. Catching a ball which is bounced will be easier than catching one which is thrown, and hitting a stationary ball will be easier than hitting one which is moving.

● Extra movement activities with an emphasis on enjoyment should lead to an improved skill level. Small-group situations are of value and should be used. The 'buddy' system may be appropriate here.

8.8 Cystic fibrosis

This is a genetically determined disorder which causes a thickening of the mucus secreted by the body, leading to reduced breathing efficiency of the lungs. It is often a deteriorating condition, and leads to problems in two main areas:

● The lungs become lined with a much thicker layer of mucus than is normal blocking the air passages.

● The mucus in the pancreas becomes thickened, thus preventing the normal flow of digestive enzymes to the small intestine. If left untreated children are not able to digest protein and fat, and may become severely malnourished.

Regular respiratory education and physiotherapy, together with modern drug: and diet supplements, have greatly improved the survival rate and lifestyles of these children.

Children with this condition cough a lot; this helps to clear the lungs.

Teachers should look out for excessive coughing, breathlessness, blueness around the lips and overtiredness. In such circumstances the child must rest.

Sometimes the sputum may be infected. The child should spit into a tissue which must be disposed of satisfactorily (down the lavatory). The hands should then be washed.

Teachers of primary-school children in particular should always have a box of tissues handy.

Teachers should also be aware of any special prescribed inhalants used by the child.

Physical education implications

● Cooperation with parents and medical advisers (particularly the child's physiotherapist) is essential for all teachers.

● Exercise is helpful, and for some children it is essential. Shorter bursts of energy may be more beneficial than endurance activities such as cross-country running. Otherwise these children should be able to participate in all aspects of physical education.

● At secondary level these children should know how much they can do and when to rest or withdraw to clear the lungs.

● At primary level the teacher's awareness of the associated problems is more critical.

● Swimming is very beneficial as it emphasises a regular and rhythmic flow of breathing. Racing, which may demand too much of the child, should not be encouraged.

● Simple trampolining is good for dislodging mucus.

● Personal physical education activities should be encouraged in order to assist the child to expand the chest and tone up chest muscles and to dislodge mucus. The following will be helpful:

○ breathing techniques — especially explosive breathing
○ postural exercises
○ heaving, swinging, pulling and pushing movements
○ trunk twisting movements

● In hot weather excessive perspiring will cause the loss of salt; this can be detrimental to the condition.

8.9 Diabetes

Diabetes is comparatively uncommon among schoolchildren. It is a condition in which the body, owing to the lack of the hormone *insulin*, is not able to absorb sugar and starch properly. Treatment is usually by means of injections of insulin and/or a controlled diet.

Physical education implications

● Children with diabetes can normally participate in most PE activities. However, because exercise can use up sugar in the blood quickly, they may need to have a suitable snack (sugar/biscuit/chocolate etc) before exercise, and sometimes afterwards.

● Strenuous activities such as swimming or cross-country running should be supervised by an informed member of staff who has supplies of sugar available in case of need.

● Careful observation is required by the teacher for symptoms of insulin reactions (*hypoglycaemia*). These are:

  ○ lack of concentration, drowsiness
  ○ shakiness, sweating
  ○ stomach ache
  ○ vomiting
  ○ untypical behaviour

The likelihood of the need for extra sugar should be established by consultation with the child's doctor and parents. It is useful for the teacher to ensure that a supply of sugar is available in case the listed symptoms occur. The child should also be encouraged to carry sugar with him/her.

8.10 Down's syndrome

Down's syndrome is a congenital condition in which the baby is born with a chromosome irregularity. The child may have unusual features (often described as mongoloid), and may be mentally retarded.

Additional handicaps such as hearing loss, poor eyesight and heart defects may also be present.

Atlanto-axial instability may also affect a small percentage of these children. In this condition the two upper cervical vertebrae of the spine are more mobile than normal. In such cases, severe pressure can produce dislocation, or may even sever the spinal cord. These children need special care — see the third point below.

Some Down's syndrome children attend mainstream schools, in particular, primary schools.

Physical education implications

● Most Down's syndrome children are able to participate in all physical education activities.

● Down's syndrome children present a wide range of physical abilities. Some will be well-coordinated and able, others will be flat-footed, overweight and clumsy.

● For pupils with atlanto-axial instability the following activities *must be avoided*:

    ○ In the gymnasium: no rolling activities, no high-level gymnastics, no trampolining
    ○ In the swimming pool: no diving, no butterfly stroke, no breast-stroke
    ○ In games and athletics: no martial arts, no boxing, no high jump

● If additional handicaps are present, these must be taken into account. (See the sections on the relevant conditions for further information.)

● Learning experiences should be well structured. Skills teaching should be broken down into simple stages of progression, and their application should be made clear.

● Defining short-term objectives is essential.

● Some children will have a very short span of concentration; reinforcement and perseverance are vital. Most children will respond to constant encouragement and praise.

8.11 Epilepsy

Epilepsy is a symptom of a disorder of the nervous system which shows itself in the form of an *epileptic seizure* (fit or attack). There are three types of attack, and the teacher should ascertain from medical or school records whether the child suffers from grand mal, petit mal, or temporal lobe epilepsy.

● *Grand mal* This is a major attack in which the child may make a strange cry fall suddenly, stiffen and then relax, before relapsing into convulsive movements. After several minutes the child should recover consciousness, although he/she will feel dazed and confused. This condition is often controlled by drugs and rarely happens at school.

● *Petit mal* is manifest by brief interruptions of consciousness and may be difficult to detect. Although brief, the absences can be frequent.

● *Temporal lobe epilepsy* This results in partial seizures taking the form of a period of partial consciousness in which abnormal behaviour such as lip-smacking, head turning and plucking at clothes may occur. These signs can be mistaken for silliness or psychological disturbances.

Physical education implications
Advice from parents and doctors should be sought. However, children with epilepsy are normally able to participate in all PE activities.

It is recommended that:

● Supervision should be provided for swimming. The child should stay in shallow water unless working alongside a responsible and informed person. Shimmering, flickering light reflected on the water may trigger an attack. Teachers should seek and respond to the advice of doctors before allowing the child to participate in swimming, and should obtain agreement from the parents. Further guidance can be obtained from the BAALPE book *Safe Practice in Physical Education*.

● Working at high levels in the gymnasium or participating in activities with elements of danger (eg rock climbing, sailing, etc) should be undertaken with extra caution, especially if the child is taking drugs and if attacks are not uncommon. As well as checking with parents and doctors, it would be a wise precaution for the teacher to ensure that the child always works with a responsible partner.

● Procedures for coping with an attack must be fully understood by the teacher:

    ○ allow the fit to take its course
    ○ cushion the head and do not restrain
    ○ do not give a drink
    ○ carefully loosen clothing around the neck
    ○ call an ambulance only if the child does not regain consciousness after fifteen minutes
    ○ after the fit, place the child in the recovery position and allow to rest

8.12 Haemophilia

Haemophilia is an inherited condition where there is life-long deficiency in a clotting factor in the blood. It is most commonly found in boys.

Children with haemophilia may bleed for much longer than normal after injury or accidental bruising. They may suffer frequent pain due to stiffness in the joints caused by internal bleeding.

Teachers should check whether normal first aid is appropriate for small cuts. Also, in such instances, teachers should pay due regard to the procedures advised by the Department of Education and Science and the Local Education Authority in respect of possible contact with the AIDS virus.

Consultation with the home over procedures for treatment following an injury or accident is essential. These children must receive prompt and correct assistance.

Physical education implications

● Most children with this condition can participate to some extent in physical education activities, and restrictions should be kept to a minimum.

● Contact sports such as rugby, soccer, basketball and netball should be avoided.

● Teachers should check with parents about the extent of participation.

● The likelihood of damage to the tissues is reduced by general fitness; swimming usually provides one of the best forms of exercise.

8.13 Hearing impairment

There are two basic types of hearing impairment: *conductive deafness* and *sensori-neural deafness*.

Conductive deafness
This affects the outer and middle ear and can result from obstruction or malformation. Most common is the occurrence of middle-ear infection caused by catarrh, fluid, inflammation, infection etc. It may be persistent or intermittent, and can often be cleared by medicine, ear drops or a simple operation.

Sensori-neural deafness
This affects the inner ear. It results from malfunction in either the inner ear or the auditory nerve, and prevents the proper transmission of sounds to the brain. Hearing loss may be permanent and severe, but in some cases may be alleviated by the use of hearing aids.

Mixed conductive and sensori-neural deafness
Some children may have a mixed conductive and sensori-neural loss.

The major factors concerning the educational implications of teaching children with hearing loss are the degree and type of loss, and the time of onset.

The personality of the children will also have a bearing on the way in which they cope with their hearing loss.

Children with a mild hearing loss are those most likely to be found in ordinary schools.

Physical education implications

● Children with partial hearing are generally allowed to participate in all activities, and this should be encouraged. However, it may be necessary to restrict certain activities such as swimming if there is middle-ear infection, a perforated ear-drum or a post-operative condition.

● Physical education is a means of internalising language and offering outlets for expression and for the non-verbal communication of ideas. Physical education makes a valuable contribution to language development.

● The child should able to see the teacher's face easily, as lip-reading will be used. The teacher should endeavour, as far as possible, to:
  ○ be near to the child
  ○ be still when speaking, and look towards the child
  ○ face the light so that his/her face is not in shadow
  ○ avoid shouting; use normal rhythm and intonation
  ○ be at the same horizontal level as the child.

- *Hearing aids.* Teachers must remember:
  - ○ when swimming — no hearing aids are to be worn
  - ○ some children will wear aids to amplify sound. Although the hearing aid is a useful tool it will not compensate fully for hearing loss
  - ○ hearing aids tend to amplify background noise and do not always make speech clearer

- Communication problems between the deaf child and the teacher can be a source of frustration to both. It is useful to devise signals whereby the child can alert the teacher to the fact that an instruction or task has not been understood.

- Normal warning signs may not be heard. The teacher should devise warning signals which deaf children can recognise and to which they will know how to respond. Another child may be designated to ensure that the hearing-impaired child knows of the warning (the 'buddy' system).

- Peripatetic teachers of the deaf are a valuable source of help and information. If difficulties arise the teacher should know how to contact the person assigned to the school.

8.14 Hydrocephalus
See Section 8.18 *Spina bifida and hydrocephalus*

8.15 Moderate learning difficulties

Many children with moderate learning difficulties are still educated in special schools. However, an increasing percentage are now benefiting from mainstream education.

This condition is not an illness or a disease. It is an intellectual impairment usually caused by genetic factors and sometimes by illness or accident.

A number of children will have additional problems such as hearing loss, poor eyesight and mild physical limitations. Some will also have emotional and behavioural difficulties. However, these children usually cope well with mainstream schooling if given the right support.

All teachers should note the following:

● learning should be well structured, with both short-term and long-term objectives clearly seen by the child

● praise and a sense of achievement are vital to motivation and self-esteem

● simple and correct sequencing and repetition are essential to the grasping of concepts and achievement of progression

● the application of learned skills may need to be taught

● concentration will be limited, and therefore short teaching sessions and varied work are important

● there will probably be a need to enhance communication and social skills, as some children will be immature in these areas

Physical education implications

● These children should be able to participate in all activities, although there will be a need to modify some approaches.

● The child with moderate learning difficulties will usually respond best in individual and small-group situations.

● Dance, gymnastics and outdoor pursuits are good activities for enhancing self-esteem and giving scope for a sense of individual achievement and creativity.

● It is important to reduce 'failure' situations as far as possible.

8.16 Muscular dystrophy

This is an inherited condition. There are several kinds, all of which are progressive. Some forms affect both sexes, but the most common — *Duchenne muscular dystrophy* — is carried through the female line and affects boys only.

The essential characteristic is a progressive breakdown of muscle fibre resulting in a gradually increasing weakness in all muscle groups. It first affects the extensor muscles of the hips, knees and shoulder girdle.

The child with muscular dystrophy coming into school at age five may have a 'waddling gait' with a sway back, and may walk on his toes. He can walk and sometimes run, but will tire easily.

The child will slowly become progressively more weak, falling more often, and finding it difficult to get up from a chair or floor, or to climb stairs.

At about eight to ten years old the child will start to use a manual wheelchair, and as the arms weaken an electric chair will be needed. Splints on the ankles and a body brace to keep the spine as straight as possible will probably be worn. At this stage the child will become prone to chest infections.

Children with muscular dystrophy should be encouraged to use all the movement they have for as long as possible. Their life expectancy now extends to the late teens and early twenties.

Physical education implications

● As the child ages, gradually lower mobility levels should be anticipated. However, these children should be included in all aspects of physical education for as long as possible.

● Teachers should appreciate that the conditions will cause children to tire easily. Some children may be prone to temper outbursts arising out of frustration.

● Adaptations to work and equipment will need to be introduced gradually and carefully to avoid frustration.

● Because of the weakness of shoulder-girdle muscles, the children can rarely use sticks or rollators. They often like to hold on to another child or walk very close to a wall.

● Swimming in warm water is one activity which can be maintained for a relatively long time. However, a close watch should be kept for tipping over onto the face — the child may not be able to return to an upright position.

● The child will need assistance from an aide or teacher in many activities, for example in dressing and undressing and getting in and out of the swimming pool. Because of the weakness of the shoulder girdle, particular care is needed:

○ do not try to lift by holding under the arms — the child will slip through your grasp
○ do not hold the hands in order to pull the child up
○ ask a physiotherapist to demonstrate correct lifting procedures

● The following activities are a few examples which teachers may find suitable for a child with muscular dystrophy:

○ swimming — very beneficial for maintaining mobility and fitness levels
○ light bat and ball games
○ archery — in a very modified form
○ wheelchair hockey
○ officiating duties

● Consultation with parents and physiotherapists is essential. The physiotherapist will be able to advise on an appropriate exercise programme to maintain fitness for as long as possible, and also on lifting and handling techniques.

8.17 Poliomyelitis

Since the introduction of an effective vaccine several decades ago, poliomyelitis has been almost wiped out in this country. However, as the number of children receiving this vaccine has recently fallen dramatically, there could be an upsurge of cases.

The disease injures the nerve circuit between the spinal cord and the peripheral nerve endings of muscles. This results in non-functioning, or partially inactive, flaccid muscles. Large or small areas of the body can be affected, leaving a variety of disabilities which may affect muscles in just one limb, or involve those in all four limbs and the trunk. There will be a loss of muscle tone and unequal muscle strengths, leading to an imbalance of the body. The deformities of some limbs may require children to wear splints, calipers or body braces.

Poor circulation in affected limbs is usual. Intellectual functioning is not affected.

Physical education implications

● Depending on the severity of the condition, many children will be able to participate in most physical education activities; however, some modifications and adaptations may be necessary.

● Swimming in warm water is particularly beneficial. The pupil should not be allowed to become cold. If the legs are affected, the supine position should be adopted first as flaccid limbs float easily.

● Those with balancing problems may be prone to falling over easily. This can be overcome to some degree by the use of aids: calipers, sticks, a body brace, etc. The physiotherapist should be able to indicate if the brace may be taken off for physical education.

● Children with an appreciable disability will begin to tire easily.

● Advice should be sought from parents and from the pupil's doctor and physiotherapist.

8.18 Spina bifida and hydrocephalus

These two conditions will often occur together, but may also occur independently. Eye defects and epilepsy are sometimes associated with spina bifida.

Spina bifida
This is a congenital condition. Where it occurs the bones of the spine (vertebrae) are incomplete and the spinal cord is exposed. The physical consequences depend on the level of the lesion (break) and the amount of damage to the spinal cord. The resulting paralysis can range from minimal to complete, and can be accompanied by partial to complete loss of sensation to the parts of the body below the level of the lesion. Sometimes there may also be spasticity in the upper limbs caused by brain damage.

Hydrocephalus
Sometimes referred to as 'water on the brain', hydrocephalus is caused by a build-up of fluid which may exert pressure on the brain. Where fluid does not drain away of its own accord, a device known as a 'shunt' is implanted to serve this purpose. Usually this will work very well, but some children will have problems with a shunt which occasionally blocks.

Physical education implications

● Spatial and/or perceptual difficulties are common. These may affect manual dexterity, hand-eye coordination and fine motor control.

● Poor motor coordination generally may cause difficulties with ball-handling skills. As with cerebral palsy, careful attention to correct sequencing will be helpful.

● Children with more severe forms of spina bifida are usually paralysed in the lower part of the body. They may move around with the aid of a wheelchair, sticks and crutches.

1 The child may wear special boots and calipers. If long leg-calipers are worn, advice about taking them on and off should be sought from a physiotherapist. If the calipers are the type worn below the knee only, most children can manage by themselves. Boots and the ferrules of sticks and rollators should be examined for wear.

● Damage to the spinal cord may cause lack of sensation to pain, temperature and touch, and also poor circulation in the lower limbs. Therefore, the following precautions should be observed by the teacher:

  ○ During sliding activities the legs and feet should be covered in order to avoid friction burns
  ○ Pressure on one part of the body over a sustained period (eg the bottom, when sitting) could cause bruising and pressure sores
  ○ Impact or scrapes on floor, apparatus and the side of the swimming bath could cause fractures

○ To avoid accidental damage, teachers' vigilance is most important: the children should be reminded to take care of the position of their legs in all activities to avoid accidental damage

● Exercise is vital to all children using wheelchairs and other aids to mobility. They should be encouraged to participate as far as they are able, in order to keep as fit and healthy as possible. Exercise aids circulation and improves muscle tone, as well as helping the functioning of many organs of the body. The child's physiotherapist should be consulted for advice on the forms of physical education which will give maximum therapeutical benefits.

● Activities which strengthen the upper body are generally considered valuable.

● Swimming is generally considered to be beneficial. Children who are paralysed in the lower limbs will often 'ride high' in the water. It is recommended, therefore, that they should start in a semi-sitting supine position. Great care of the limbs should be exercised when entering and leaving the water to avoid scrapes and bangs; the pool water should be warm.

● *Incontinence* Many children with the more severe form of spina bifida are incontinent of the bowels and/or bladder. Some have surgery to bypass the bowel or bladder, and others use a catheter to drain urine. It is useful for the child and the teacher to have a spare pair of shorts or tracksuit trousers available in case of accidents.

Advice on special arrangements should be sought before proceeding with any physical activity.

Time, privacy and perhaps assistance will be needed. Some children will be able to manage their toilet arrangements quite independently, but it may be necessary to provide a private changing area.

● Children with hydrocephalus may have a slightly enlarged head which will be quite heavy, so they should not be rushed.

● *Health notes*:

○ If a child with hydrocephalus develops a severe headache, drowsiness or vomiting, this may indicate that the shunt is not working properly
○ A high temperature may be indicative of a urinary infection

In either of these cases the parents should be contacted immediately.

Special considerations, modifications and adaptations may be necessary. However, many children with spina bifida, hydrocephalus, or both conditions in combination are able to participate satisfactorily in most physical education activities.

8.19 Visual impairment

Functional loss of vision may be considered in two categories:

● problems associated with *focus*. These may often be remedied or assisted by spectacles or other appropriate aids, but some conditions cannot be corrected.

● problems associated with the *field of vision*. These may be either peripheral problems, or problems within the field of vision.

Peripheral vision is important for mobility and for the perception of moving objects. It is used for scanning the environment and detecting moving objects.

Within the field of normal vision all people have a blind spot on the retina of the eye which cannot receive visual images. Sometimes these areas are larger than normal and hence vision may be hazy and/or fragmented.

Common eye faults

● *myopia* (short sight)

● *hypermetropia* (long sight)

● *astigmatism* (unevenness of focal deflection)

The above three faults can usually be corrected by the wearing of spectacles.

● *squints* (imbalance of pupil convergence)

● *hemianopia* − a reduction of the usual field of vision, producing either tunnel vision, peripheral vision or the inability to see that which is on one side. This is common in cases of hemiplegia.

● *glaucoma* − excessive pressure of the fluid within the eyeball. Leads to a progressive loss of the field of vision, which can be halted if detected early enough.

● *cataract* − opacity of the lens which leads to a reduction in the amount of light which can enter the eye. This can usually be corrected by spectacles or surgery.

● *colour blindness*. Total colour blindness is rare. The more common form, affecting 8% of males and 1% of females, is really colour deficiency, resulting in an inability to distinguish certain colours, generally red and green.

Physical education implications

● Apart from the more obvious implications, eye defects are variously responsible for difficulties in coordination, orientation, position in space, object identification and tracking.

- Spectacles should be worn in physical education lessons if the child finds that they are helpful. They should have shatterproof lenses, and should be secured.

- Good light is important.

- *Swimming*:

  - In instances where the wearing of spectacles poses problems, the child should be well informed of the geography of the pool: the depth, width and length, entry and exit points, rails and troughs. Orientation is easier in the prone position than in the supine.
  - In certain cases the teacher should obtain medical approval before allowing the child to enter chlorinated water.

- Safe practice in all activities should be fully understood by the child. The teacher must be aware that the partially sighted child will not necessarily see dangerous situations or stray missiles.

- Games which involve the use of small balls may prove difficult if vision and/or hand–eye coordination are poor. Using brightly coloured balls may be helpful.

- The placement of apparatus and equipment should be as constant as possible. Any changes from the normal practice should be made clear to the visually impaired child. Unnecessary equipment must be tidied away and not left lying about in a haphazard fashion.

- Partially-sighted children need to be as independent as possible, but it is often useful to designate friends to assist them without taking away their confidence.

- Teachers should be able to obtain advice on suitable strategies for assisting the partially-sighted child in physical education from the peripatetic teacher specially assigned to the school.

Chapter Nine

Glossary of Medical Terms

Abduction   Movement of a limb outward and away from the mid-line of the body, eg raising an arm or leg out to one side.

Achilles tendon   The 'heel-cord': the long tendon which joins the calf muscles to the heel. The achilles tendon can easily be felt at the back of the heel.

Adaptive behaviour   Behaviour that aids the individual in effective, independent social function.

Adduction   The opposite of *abduction*. Movement of a limb inward and towards, or even across, the mid-line of the body.

Aetiology   The study of the causes of a disease.

Agnosia   An inability to recognise objects or sounds due to lack of perceptive capacity, although the general level of intelligence is normal.

Aphasia   A specific defect of brain function which leads to a person being unable to express ideas in words, or being unable to understand spoken language.

Apraxia   An inability to perform purposeful movements which is not accompanied by any apparent muscular weakness. A typical example would be the inability to use a screwdriver. Apraxia is due to a dysfunction of the brain.

Arteriosclerosis   Thickening or hardening of the walls of the blood vessels, particularly the arteries.

Arthredesis   A surgical operation to fix a joint in one position.

Ataxia   A generalised incoordination of movement due to incoordination of the muscles involved. This results in instability of sitting, standing and walking, and a similar disturbance of arm movement.

Athetosis   The result of a certain type of brain lesion. The term is used to indicate a particular sort of uncontrollable movement and posture which prevents or seriously impairs normal movement. It is present in the *athetoid* type of cerebral palsy.

Atonic   Term used to describe diminished resistance to passive movements of the segments of the limbs of a patient.

Atrophy   Wasting away, or reduction in size — very often applied to muscles.

Audiogram   A record of the hearing acuity of a patient, in the form of a graph.

Audiometer   Instrument used to test hearing acuity at different frequency levels and intensities.

Catheter   A tube used for evacuating fluid from the bladder.

Cerebral palsy   A disorder of movement and posture arising in the early years of life as a result of some interference with the normal development of the brain. It is non-progressive in that the damage to the brain itself will not get worse, although the symptoms may change from time to time.

Circumduction   Circular movement of a limb.

Contra-indications   Signs or symptoms which indicate against the use of a particular treatment or training method.

Diplegia   Weakness (*paresis*) of the upper and lower limbs of both sides of the body. Diplegia is usually understood to imply that the lower limbs are more severely affected than the upper (cf *double hemiplegia*).

Distractibility   The inability to concentrate. A person who is easily distracted from the performance of a task suffers from distractibility.

Dislocation   Displacement of organs or joint surfaces.

Distal   Situated away from the centre of the body or point of attachment.

Double hemiplegia   *Paresis* involving the limbs on both sides of the body — with the upper limbs more severely affected than the lower.

Down's syndrome   A specific set of symptoms associated with mental retardation, previously often referred to as *mongolism*. The cause is genetic.

Dyslexia   Difficulty in reading due to a defect of brain function other than sensory defect. The alternative word *alexia* is sometimes used.

Epilepsy   A condition which causes a person to suffer from fits characterised by abnormal and uncontrollable movements of the body, and unconsciousness. Such fits are described as *grand mal* when there is a loss of consciousness and convulsions, or as *petit mal* when there is only momentary loss of consciousness and no convulsions.

Eversion   The process of turning outwards.

Extension   The process of straightening a flexed part.

Extensor   The name given to those muscles which, when they contract, cause a joint to straighten.

Flexion   The process of bending.

Flexor   The name given to those muscles which, when they contract, cause a joint to bend (or flex).

Grand mal   See *epilepsy*.

Hemiplegia   Weakness or paralysis of the limbs on one side of the body as the result of a disorder of the brain.

Hydrocephaly   A condition in which spinal fluid is trapped in the cranial area, creating pressure on the brain. This usually causes retardation.

Hyperkinesis   Incessant restless activity.

Hypertension   Tension or muscle tone above normal.

Ileostomy   An opening in the abdominal wall; a surgical passage.

Incontinence   Inability to retain urine or faeces.

Inversion   The process of turning inwards.

Kinaesthesia   The sense and understanding of where one's limbs are, including whether still or in motion.

Laterality   Having to do with the side; a knowledge of left and right.

Mongolism   See *Down's syndrome.*

Monoplegia   *Paresis* or paralysis affecting one limb only.

Muscle tone   Degree of tension in muscle when the muscle is in a resting state.

Neurological   Pertaining to nerve function.

Orthopaedics   The study of deformities and diseases of the joints and bones.

Osteomyelitis   Inflammation of the bone, especially the marrow.

Paralysis   Strictly speaking *paralysis* means complete palsy, resulting in inability to move a particular part of the body. Many people misuse *paralysis* to describe weakness only; see also *paresis.*

Paraplegia   Weakness or paralysis affecting the legs only.

Paresis   Weakness or partial paralysis, affecting muscular motion but not sensation.

Petit mal   See *epilepsy.*

Physiological   Concerning the study of the working of the body and its parts.

Polio   *Poliomyelitis* — a disease causing inflammation of the spinal cord, often leading to *paresis.*

Prone   Lying in a face-down position.

Prosthetic device   An artificial limb or device attached to the limbs; an artificial organ or body part.

Psychosis   A mental illness, other than intellectual handicap (sub-normality), in which the patient does not have insight. Children suffering from a psychosis do not understand that their minds are not working properly. A psychosis is a more severe and fundamental illness than a neurosis, and is characterised by greater disorganisation of behaviour, particularly in relationships with other people.

Pulmonary   Having to do with the pulmonary artery; concerning heart-valve function or lung function.

Quadriplegia   Weakness or paralysis affecting all four limbs. See also *tetraplegia*.

Reflex   A stereotyped automatic movement made without conscious effort, such as the sudden withdrawal of the hand when pricked with a pin, or the jerk of the lower leg when the knee is tapped.

Rehabilitation   Restoration of a disabled person to the fullest possible functioning.

Reinforcement   A reinforcement is anything that increases the likelihood of a behaviour pattern being repeated.

Retarded   A word used to indicate physical or intellectual development which is less than average for a person of the same age. Often used to indicate suspected mental subnormality or as a euphemism for *mentally subnormal*.

Rigidity   Sustained stiffness of a limb or limbs in extension.

Scoliosis   Curvature of the spine.

Self-image   Concept of or belief about self.

Seizure   Spasmodic muscular contractions; a convulsion.

Sensory   Having to do with that part of the nervous system which receives and interprets signals through the *senses*, as distinct from *motor* which has to do with that part of the nervous system which transmits signals to the muscles and so organises the activities of the body.

Spastic   A term with two meanings:

● Popularly used to indicate any child or adult suffering from *cerebral palsy*.

● Used medically to describe a specific type of stiffness commonly seen in the limbs in *hemiplegia* and *diplegia*. This is detected by the particular sort of increase in resistance to passive movement of the parts of the limb.

Spasticity   The state of being *spastic*.

Spatial perception   The appreciation of size and distance, and of the relation-ship of objects to one another.

Stimulus   Any agent or factor able to influence or elicit a response.

Supine Lying in a face-up position.

Talipes The medical word for clubfoot.

Tetraplegia Weakness or paralysis affecting all four limbs. See also *paraplegia*.

Tonic Sustained tension in a limb.

Trauma An injury, wound, or painful emotional experience.

Tremor Rhythmic, uncontrolled repetitive movement of parts of the body.

Triplegia Weakness or paralysis affecting three limbs.

Valgus, varus Terms used to describe the position of a limb *distal* to the joint under consideration. If the part beyond the joint points away from the mid-line, there is said to be a *valgus* joint. If it points towards the mid-line the joint is said to be *varus*.

Voluntary muscles Muscles under the control of the will.

Chapter Ten
Resources

10.1 Bibliography

General publications

Berridge and Ward (edited); *Adapted physical activity*; Human Kinetics (USA)

Bilbrough A and Jones P; *Physical Education in the primary school*; University of London Press

Chartered Society of Physiotherapists; *Handling the handicapped*; Woodhead Faulkner

Churcher B; *Physical education for teaching*; Unwin

Croucher N; *Joining in − integrated sport and leisure for the disabled*; Disabilities Studies Unit

Croucher N; *Outdoor pursuits for disabled people*; Disabled Living Foundation

Department of Education and Science; *Movement − physical education in primary years*; HMSO

Department of Education and Science; *Physical education for the physically handicapped*; HMSO

Department of Education and Science; *Special educational needs (Warnock Report)*; HMSO

Duke of Edinburgh's Award Scheme; *No handicap*; Duke of Edinburgh's Award Office

Eason Smith C; *Adapted physical activity − theory to application*; Human Kinetics (USA)

George S J and Hart B; *Physical education for handicapped children*; Souvenir

Groves L (editor); *Physical education for children with special needs*; Cambridge University Press

Guttmann L; *Textbook of sport for the disabled*; John Wiley and Sons

Hayle G (editor); *Source book for the disabled*; Muller

Illingworth R S; *The development of the infant and young child − normal and abnormal*; Livingstone

Latto K; *Give us the chance − physical activities and sport for mentally handicapped children*; Disabled Living Foundation

Mandelstam D; *Incontinence*; Heinemann

Mortimore F; *Making movement fun*; National Society for Mentally Handicapped Children

National Coaching Foundation; *Play the game*; NCF

Price R J; *Physical education and the physically handicapped child*; Lepus

Robinson C M et al; *Physical activities in the education of slow-learning children*; Edward Arnold

Scout Book Shops; *Extension activities — a handbook for trainers of handicapped scouts*; SBS

Stuart F; *Leisure for mentally handicapped people*; National Society for Mentally Handicapped Children

Upton G (editor); *Physical and creative activities for the mentally handicapped*; Cambridge University Press

Winnick J and Short F; *Physical fitness testing of the disabled*; Human Kinetics (USA)

Local education authority publications

British Association of Advisers and Lecturers in Physical Education; *Local education authority publications on physical education*; BAALPE

Coventry LEA; *Physical education for nursery and infant pupils*; Coventry Education Committee

Kent LEA; *Physical education for pupils with special educational needs in mainstream schools*; Kent County Council, Maidstone

Lancashire LEA; *Lancashire looks at physical education in the special school*; Lancashire County Council, Preston

Activity-specific publications

GYMNASTICS

Allen J E; *Sense and sensitivity in gymnastics*; Heinemann

Bilbrough A and Jones P; *Physical education in the primary school*; University of London Press

British Amateur Gymnastics Association; *Gymnastics for schools*; BAGA

Cameron W McD and Cameron M; *Education and movement in the infant school*; Blackwell

Cameron W McD and Pleasance P; *Education in movement — school gymnastics*; Blackwell

Learmouth J and Whittaker K; *Movement in practice*; Schofield and Sims

Long B; *Educational gymnastics step by step*; Edward Arnold

Mauldon E and Layson J; *Teaching gymnastics*; MacDonald and Evans

Morison R; *A movement approach to educational gymnastics*; Dent

Williams J; *Themes for educational gymnastics*; Lepus

DANCE

Allcock and Bland; *Dance in education*; Dance Books

Bruce V; *Dance and dance drama in education*; Pergamon

Bruce V; *Lord of the dance*; Pergamon

Carroll J and Lofthouse P; *Creative dance for boys*; MacDonald and Evans

Driver A; *Music and movement*; Oxford University Press

Gray V and Percival R; *Music, movement and mime for children*; Oxford University Press

Hertfordshire LEA; *Expressive movement and dance*; Hertfordshire Education Committee

Levete G; *No handicap to dance*; Souvenir

Lofthouse P; *Dance*; Heinemann

Russell J; *Creative dance in the primary school*; MacDonald and Evans

Russell J; *Modern dance in education*; Macdonald and Evans

Sheehy; *Children discover music and dance*; Teachers College Press

Shreeves; *Children dancing*; Ward Lock

Smedley R and Tether J; *Let's dance — country style*; Paul Elek

Smith J; *Dance composition*; Lepus

Staffordshire LEA; *Dance*; Staffordshire Education Committee

White T; *Visual poetry for creative interpretation*; MacDonald and Evans

GAMES

Almond L, Bunker D and Thorpe R; *Games for understanding*; Loughborough University of Technology

Brown A; *Active games for children with movement problems*; Paul Chapman

Football Association; *Play the game of soccer*; FA and National Coaching Foundation

Frith J R and Lobley R; *Playground games and skills*; A and C Black

Johnson F and Trevor M; *A suggested games scheme for juniors*; Blackwell

Lee C; *The playground lesson*; Bell

Lenel R M; *Games in the primary school*; University of London Press

Maulden E and Redfern A B; *Games teaching – a new approach for the primary school*; MacDonald and Evans

Sleap M; *Mini-sport*; Heinemann

Various; *Know the game* books; A and C Black

Wise W M; *Games and sport*; Heinemann

SWIMMING

Amateur Swimming Association; *The teaching of swimming*; ASA

American Red Cross; *Adapted aquatics*; available from ASA

Anderson W; *Teaching the physically handicapped to swim*; Faber and Faber

Association of Swimming Therapy; *Swimming for the disabled*; EP

Committee on Swimming for the Disabled; *Lifting and handling, swimming and epilepsy – medical considerations*; Sports Council

Reid M J; *Handling the disabled child in water*; Association of Chartered Pediatric Physiotherapists

Royal Life Saving Society; *Life saving and water safety*; RLSS

Trussell E; *Guidelines for teaching the disabled to swim*; Swimming Teachers Association

OUTDOOR PURSUITS

Blackshaw A; *Mountaineering*; Penguin

Bond B; *The sailing manual*; Pelham

Byde A; *Living canoeing*; Black

Croucher N; *Outdoor pursuits for disabled people*; Disabled Living Foundation

Department of Education and Science; *Safety in outdoor pursuits*; HMSO

Disley J; *Orienteering*; Faber and Faber

Parker T M and Meldrum K I; *Outdoor education*; Dent

Riding for the Disabled Association; *Riding for the disabled handbook*; RDA, Kenilworth

Sports Council; *Water sports for the disabled*; RYA Seamanship Foundation

10.2 Videos and films

The following films are available from **Town and Country Productions Ltd,** 21 Cheyne Row, Chelsea, London SW3 5HP; tel 01-352 7950.

Not just a spectator; Disabled Living Foundation (1974). An inspirational film showing a wide range of activities and sports for people with different disabilities. Commentary by Robert Dougall.
Colour 35 minutes

I want to be; Invalid Children's Aid Association. Examines the many problems that face handicapped children and their families. Reference is made to individual case studies.
16mm colour/sound 35 minutes

Able to fish; Disabled Living Foundation in cooperation with the National Anglers' Council (1977). Three films showing how sea, coarse and game fishing can be made available to disabled persons of all ages, how special tackle has been designed, and where they may fish in safety.

Riding towards freedom; Riding for the Disabled Association. A description of how a new centre for handicapped riders is established by cooperation between volunteers, physiotherapists and members of the medical profession.
16mm colour/sound 35 minutes

The right to choose; Riding for the Disabled Association. Shows how riding can help people with disabilities such as paraplegia, amputation and paralysis.
16mm colour/sound 30 minutes

Water free; Association of Swimming Therapy. Shows methods of coaching disabled people to swim and dive. Also shows the potential of the Halliwick method of swimming instruction for the teacher of handicapped children.
16mm colour/sound 35 minutes

Give us the chance; Disabled Living Foundation (1983). Shows how mentally handicapped children can participate successfully and with enjoyment in a wide range of sports and physical activities.
35 minutes

The following group of films is available from **Concord Film Council Ltd,** Nacton, Ipswich, Suffolk IP10 0JZ; tel Ipswich (0473) 726012.

In touch — movement for mentally handicapped children; produced on behalf of the National Association for Mental Health.
16mm black-and-white/sound 30 minutes

A sense of movement — movement for severely retarded children.
16mm colour 40 minutes

Explorations; shows work with the mentally handicapped.
16mm black-and-white 30 minutes

Moving and lifting a disabled person.
16mm colour/sound 13 minutes

Special Olympics; shows how mentally handicapped people can overcome their disability and join in sporting activities with joy.
16mm colour/sound

Films from other sources

It's a new world; shows potential achievements of those with differing abilities. Some of the swimmers from the Olympic Games for the Disabled.
16mm colour/sound 30 minutes
Available from: National Audio-Visual Aids Library, Paxton Place, Gypsy Road, London SE7 9SR.

An adventure playground for the handicapped.
16mm colour/sound
Catalogue no 3099. Available from: Central Film Library, Government Building, Bromyard Avenue, Acton, London W3 7JB; tel 01-743 5555.

It's ability that counts (1975).
16mm colour 25 minutes
Hire from: The Administrator, BSAD, Stoke Mandeville Sports Stadium, Harvey Road, Aylesbury, Bucks.

So we're different but...?; Central Office of Information for the DES. Examines the role of the special school in educating the physically handicapped to achieve and accept the fine balance which must exist between dependence and independence. Shows participation in a variety of physical activities.
16mm colour/sound 31 minutes
Available from: Central Film Library, Bromyard Avenue, London W3 7BJ.

I can dance; Manchester Education Authority. Shows adolescent ESN(M) girls dancing in response to a variety of stimuli.
16mm colour/sound 15 minutes
Available from: The Visual Aids Department, Education Offices, Crown Square, Manchester M60 3BB.

10.3 Organisations and addresses

National coordinating organisations

British Amputees Sports Association, John Fisher, 7 Douglas Road, Harpenden, Herts. Tel. (0582) 460105

British Association for Sporting and Recreational Activities of the Blind, Ian Fell, Secretary, 2 Westwood Road, Hillmorton, Rugby CV22 5QL. Tel. (0788) 65604

British Deaf Sports Council, Mr Roland Haythornethwaite, Administrator, Office Suite No. 1, 54 Boroughgate, Otley, West Yorkshire, LS21 1AE. Tel. (0943) 462917

British Les Autres Sports Association, M W Pattison, 30 Greaves Close, Arnold, Nottingham, NG5 6RS. Tel. (0602) 260220

British Paraplegic Sports, Sir Ludwig Guttmann Sports Centre, Harvey Road, Aylesbury, Bucks, HP21 8PP. Tel. (0296) 84848

British Sports Association for the Disabled Limited, Dr R J Price, Director and Chief Executive, Hayward House, Barnard Crescent, Aylesbury, Bucks, HP21 9PP. Tel. (0296) 27889

Cerebral Palsy International Sports and Recreation Association (CP Sports), Spastics Society, 16 Fitzroy Square, London W1P 5HQ. Tel. 01-387 9571

Disabled Living Foundation, Elizabeth Fanshawe, Director, 380/384 Harrow Road, London W9 2HU. Tel. 01-289 6111. Keeps up-to-date list of all books, films and videos concerned about the disabled, with particular reference to physical activity.

Handicapped Adventure Playground Association, Fulham Palace, Bishops Avenue, London SW6 6EA. Tel. 01-736 4443

Special Olympics U.K. (Mental Handicap), Willesborough Industrial Park, Kennington Road, Willesborough, Ashford, Kent TN22 0TD. Tel. (0233) 39910

United Kingdom Sports Association for People with a Mental Handicap, Mark Southam, 1st Floor, Unit 9, Longlands Industrial Estate, Milner Way, Ossett, Wakefield, WF5 9JN. Tel. (0924) 279305

Other useful addresses

Amateur Swimming Association, D Reeves, Secretary, Harold Fern House, Derby Square. Loughborough, Leics LE11 0AL. Tel. (0509) 230431

Association of Swimming Therapy, Ted Cowen, 4 Oak Street, Shrewsbury, Shropshire SY3 7RH. Tel. (0743) 4393

British Disabled Water Ski Association, Mrs M Edge, Secretary, 18 Greville Park Avenue, Ashtead, Surrey KT21 2QS. Tel. (0372) 273046

British Judo Association Working Party for the Disabled, British Judo Association, 16 Upper Woburn Place, London WC1H 0QH. Tel. 01-387 9340

British Ski Club for the Disabled, H Sturges, Chairman, Corton House, Corton, Near Warminster, Wiltshire BA12 0SZ. Tel. (0985) 50321

Calvert Trust (Challenge for the Disabled) Ltd, The Calvert Trust, Little Crosthwaite, Underskiddaw, Keswick, Cumbria CA12 4QD. Tel. (0596) 72254

Diamond Centre for Handicapped Riders, Woodmansterne Road, Carshalton, Surrey SM5 4DT. Tel. 01-643 7764

Duke of Edinburgh's Award Scheme, Award Offices, 5 Prince of Wales Terrace, London W8 5PG. Tel. 01-937 5205

Elfrida Rathbone Association, 22 Yonge Park, Finsbury Park, London N4 3NT. Tel. 01-607 8157 [Clubs for ESN(M)].

English National Association of Visually Handicapped Bowlers, G Rawlinson, Hon.Sec., 11 Wordsworth Road, Clevedon, Avon BS21 6PQ. Tel. (0272) 875969

Great Britain Wheelchair Basketball League, David Foden, Chairman, 14 Hannerton Road, Shaw, Oldham, Lancs. Tel. (0706) 842820 [home] 061-652 1176 [work]

Jubilee Sailing Trust, Test Road, Eastern Docks, Southampton SO1 1GG. Tel. (0703) 631388

National Association of Swimming Clubs for the Handicapped, Alan Thornton, National Co-ordinator, St George's House, Coventry Road, Coleshill, Birmingham B46 3ED. Tel. (0675) 63709

National Star Centre for Disabled Youth, Ullen Wood Manor, Cheltenham, Gloucestershire, GL50 1PE. Tel. (0242) 527631

National Wheelchair Dance Association, Mrs J M Boyle, Secretary, 30 Templar Road, Preston, Paignton, Devon TQ3 1EL. Tel. (0803) 522138

Physically Handicapped and Able-Bodied Residential and Clubs Movement (PHAB), Tavistock House North, Tavistock Square, London WC1H 9HX. Tel. 01-388 1963

Riding for the Disabled Association, R Moss, Director, Avenue 'R', National Agricultural Centre, Stoneleigh, Kenilworth, Warwickshire, CV8 2LY. Tel. (0203) 56107

Scout Book Shops, Churchill Industrial Estate, Lancing, Sussex BN15 8UG. Tel. (0903) 755352

SHAPE (Movement and Dance) 9 Fitzroy Square, London W1P 6AE. Tel. 01-388 9622

Society for One-armed Golfers, 11 Coldwell Lane, Felling, Tyne & Wear NE10 9EX (0632). Tel. 694742

Wheelchair Fencing Association, 14 Kingsley Park Grove, Sheffield S11 9HL. Tel. (0742) 362194